Always Present

Always Present

The Luminous Wisdom of
JIGME PHUNTSOK

Edited by
KHENPO SODARGYE

SNOW LION
Boston & London
2015

Snow Lion
An imprint of Shambhala Publications, Inc.
Horticultural Hall
300 Massachusetts Avenue
Boston, Massachusetts 02115
www.shambhala.com

9 8 7 6 5 4 3 2 1

First Edition
Printed in the United States of America
♾ This edition is printed on acid-free paper that meets the
American National Standards Institute z39.48 Standard.
♻ This book is printed on 30% postconsumer recycled paper.
For more information please visit www.shambhala.com.
Distributed in the United States by Penguin Random House LLC
and in Canada by Random House of Canada Ltd

LIBRARY OF CONGRESS CATALOGING-IN-PUBLICATION DATA
'Jigs-med-phun-tshogs-'byun-gnas, 1933–2004, author.
[Bu li. English]
Always present: the luminous wisdom of Jigme Phuntsok / edited by
Khenpo Sodargye.—First edition.
pages   cm
Previously published in Chinese by Sino-Culture Press.
ISBN 978-1-55939-450-5 (paperback)
1. Spiritual life—Rñin-ma-pa (Sect) I. Suodaji, Kanbu, 1962– II. Title.
BQ7662.6.J5413 2015
294.3D444—dc23
2014031065

Do not lose your own path.
Do not disturb others' minds.

Contents

Editor's Preface

Ten years have passed since our teacher His Holiness Jigme Phuntsok Rinpoche departed from us. The days I spent by our teacher's side were the most wonderful days of my life, and they remain my most extraordinary memories. No matter where he went or what the ethnicity of his audience, whether he taught the profound Buddhadharma or spoke about ordinary, everyday life, people received great benefit.

I once heard someone say, "His Holiness is noble, but he does not tower over you at all with his words or actions. His gentleness and humility allow each person nearby to feel happy and warm." I always found this to be true. Like the Buddha, His Holiness benefited beings by living and teaching the Dharma. Through the Buddhadharma, he led us to see ourselves clearly, realize the truth of all things, and find the path of liberation.

During the Cultural Revolution, Buddhism was devastated. After ten years of catastrophe, His Holiness revitalized Tibetan Buddhism in China. To this day, no other Tibetan master has taken on so many Han Chinese students of the fourfold sangha—monks, nuns, lay women, and lay men.

From 1987 until His Holiness's *parinirvana** in early 2004, I assumed the role of his Mandarin interpreter and served at his side as his attendant. Regrettably, due to various causes and conditions over those eighteen years, only a few of His Holiness's teachings were preserved.

On the occasion of the tenth anniversary of His Holiness's parinirvana, I began an exhaustive search through the recordings of the teachings he gave both at home and abroad. From these, I selected some teachings and translated them as an offering to all who have an affinity with His Holiness. As the First Dodrupchen Jigme Trinle Özer prophesied over two hundred years ago, any being that forms a connection with His Holiness Jigme Phuntsok Rinpoche can be reborn in a pure land of great bliss. It is therefore auspicious that His Holiness's teachings are now being shared in this book.

Whether you are a student of the Buddha or not, when you open this book, you will benefit from it.

Each word and phrase in the book is His Holiness's vajra speech, unadulterated by my own discriminating thoughts. All of His Holiness's direct disciples, who are as numerous as the stars, can attest to this.

Some teachings in the book are quite pointed, which may lead some readers to feel like they are sitting on a bed of needles. But just as the Venerable Atisha said, "Criticisms that hit the mark are the most sublime teachings. Masters who admonish their disciples' wrongdoings are the best mentors." Truly, those who love you most are the ones who are willing

---

* Parinirvana (Skt.): The passing away of a buddha or highly realized master.

to be honest with you about your mistakes. Whenever His Holiness censured students, it was like a loving mother's reproach of an errant child. His criticism arose entirely from compassion and kindness.

In this day and age, many people have never before encountered or heard teachings like these that open the ears of the deaf and the eyes of the blind. You have the great fortune to encounter them. These are teachings to be treasured.

May this book be an eternal lamp, forever illuminating your path ahead.

SODARGYE
Tibetan Year of the Water Snake
January 2014

Always Present

Introduction

Homage to our original teacher Shakyamuni Buddha!

It is said in the sutras, "Rare is birth as a human being, and difficult it is to obtain the chance to listen to the Dharma." In the vast, limitless sea of samsara, most people squander their precious lives in completely meaningless worldly activities. Only a scarce few can rely on the right teachings to tame their minds. To be born as a human and to study and practice the Buddhadharma without wasting one's years is even more rare. We should feel immeasurable joy that we have the good fortune to listen to this Dharma.

When listening to Buddhadharma, respect and wisdom are very important. Without respect, we cannot value the vajra speech of the Buddha, of eminent monks, and of great masters. No matter how sublime the Buddhadharma, we could not possibly obtain a drop of benefit. Without wisdom, we could not earnestly reflect and deliberate, and so we could not truly realize the profound meanings of the Dharma.

Thus, only with the miraculous tongue of respect and wisdom can one taste the sublime nectar of the Buddhadharma and dispel the burning afflictions in the mind!

I

Why We Are Not Happy

THOUGHTS ARE LIKE misty clouds in the sky.
If we abide in a natural state of being, thoughts
provide no help and do no harm. Once discriminative thoughts or attachments arise, they hold
myriad harms and not a single benefit.

What Truly Torments You
Is the Demon of the Mind

The Buddha's teachings often refer to the "demon king" as
one of the four demons. In general, people believe this refers to Mara, but in fact, the real demon is our ignorance and
confusion.

This demon king hides constantly in the dark corner of
delusion. To obstruct us from obtaining eternal peace and
happiness, he continually shoots the five arrows: craving,
anger, stinginess, pride, and envy. These cause such fierce
suffering that anyone who is shot by them would rather die
than live. The supreme antidote that dispels this daily harm
is to realize the nature of all phenomena. This is none other

than the sword of wisdom held by the bodhisattva Manjushri.

Each one of us, even in our dreams, aspires to be peaceful and happy, safe and sound, and free from pain and suffering. But in reality, no one can bestow this upon us. Some people in this world enjoy limitless happiness, while others experience severe suffering. Does this huge difference occur and shift according to people's own wishes? The answer is evidently no, because no one would willingly suffer.

Take wealth, for example. Most people wish for it, rather than hope for poverty. But if there was no accumulated merit and fortune in your past lives, then even though you thirst for wealth and desperately seek it in this life, the outcome will probably not be as you wish.

Of course, if there truly were a creator of suffering, then it would be perfectly reasonable to hate him or her to the marrow. But if we seek the perpetrator of our sufferings in external circumstances, we will not find one. Such a search will inevitably be in vain.

What truly torments us is actually an inner demon king. Insidiously, he hides in our mind, eluding discovery. Day and night he shadows us, so it is very easy for him to destroy us. Under his repressive hand, we are like slaves with no freedom at all, and we continually experience all manner of misery.

But the greatest tragedy is that most of the time we have no idea who is playing tricks on us. So exterminating him is as difficult as soaring in the skies.

Your Suffering Is in Direct Proportion to Your Pride,
Craving, Anger, Stinginess, and Ignorance

The demon king hides in the deepest part of our heart and continually shoots the five arrows, also called the flower arrows. They are lovely to look at, so we can't help yearning for them. But as soon as they pierce our heart, we tremble with great suffering.

These five flower arrows are also known as the five great demons emanated from the demon king. We should carefully identify them, and we must not take them lightly.

The one that can cast us into a very degraded state is called the demon of pride.

When one yearns for a man or a woman, or for anything with a beautiful appearance—a form, sound, smell, taste, or touch—that causes the mind to be fettered, this is called the demon of craving.

The one that can lead us into the three lower realms is the demon of stinginess.

The one that completely destroys our own and others' virtue is the demon of anger.

The one that leads us to feel competitive with others, hoping they never attain fame or fortune, and also to slander them, is called the demon of envy.

Since time without beginning, these demons have been tormenting us constantly. They have brought us unspeakable pain and suffering. If you can clearly see this one day soon, I believe that no matter who you are, you will not wish to live with these great enemy afflictions for even a moment.

Of course, the leader of these five demons is none other than the demon king—the demon of ignorance. Only when you have opened the eyes of wisdom can you completely eliminate his influence. Alternatively, you can first use the sword of wisdom to strike down all of the demon king's five emanations. Then the demon king will lose the power to resist and can only yield meekly.

Thus, whether we follow the path of the Sutrayana or the Vajrayana, the most fundamental point is to realize the nature of mind. Only then will all the demons have nowhere to hide and naturally disperse.

Craving Is All in Vain

We should not crave any person or thing, either material or immaterial. Why? Because if you observe the nature of those external objects that you crave and desire, you will find that they are like bubbles and have no true essence. What is there to crave?

Once you find that external objects have no true existence, look inward to observe your mind, and you will find that it also does not exist. Each thought that arises in the mind appears real, vivid, true, and solid. But if you carefully dissect a thought, you will discover its fleeting nature. It is born in this moment and dies in this moment. Its nature is like empty space and cannot be found anywhere.

Since craved objects do not exist, nor does a mind that craves, how could craving possibly arise?

You might wonder, "If craving does not essentially exist, why do I still crave?" This situation is really very unfortunate. Due to the obscuration of ignorance, worldly people regard things that do not essentially exist to be real. This ignorance continually produces attachments, afflictions, and suffering. In short, this is entirely a matter of being caught in one's own trap and reaping the fruits of one's own actions.

Of course, it is not nearly enough just to understand the empty nature of craving—we must also realize it. Similarly, when a person only theoretically knows how to drive a car but has never actually done it, we cannot say that he or she really knows how to drive.

Buddhism provides many methods to attain realization. You can use the Middle Way (*madhyamaka*) methods of reasoning and inquiry, or use the pith instructions of the Great Seal (*mahamudra*) and Great Perfection (*dzogchen*) and draw upon the blessings of your teacher to see the nature of mind. No matter which method you adopt, you must remember that although all phenomena in the ultimate dimension are of the nature of emptiness, you must not become attached even to emptiness!

Greed Leads to Poverty

Some people hate to use their wealth even for their own enjoyment, much less share it with anyone else. When these people face death, their miserly nature becomes an immense obstacle to liberation, so much so that they could even be reborn as hungry ghosts. Even if they are reborn as humans, they will inevitably suffer constant poverty, and for life after life they will have no possibility for wealth. Therefore, we must do everything possible to eliminate stinginess.

Forgive Your Enemy as You Would Forgive Your Own Mother

No matter who our enemies are and no matter how they've harmed us, we should not bear anger toward them. Instead, as much as possible, we should visualize them as our own mothers and cultivate compassion and loving-kindness toward them.

It is taught widely in Buddhist texts that since beginningless time, every living being in samsara has been our mother, who endured all kinds of hardships to nurture us, cared for us with the greatest love, and gave us everything that she held dear. We owe a debt of gratitude as weighty as a mountain to these mothers of the past. Yet by the cruel trick of karma, they no longer remember us in this lifetime and have even become our enemies. If it were in our mother's power, she could not possibly wish to cause us suffering.

Think back to a time when you were ill, and tell yourself, "No matter how rude and unreasonable my behavior, my mother showed the greatest concern and tended me lovingly in many ways, without any complaint. Yet today, because she has been drifting for so long in the unbearably bitter sea of samsara, she is unfortunately 'ill' and no longer recognizes me. Now that she has nothing and no one to rely on, how could I, because of some slight hurt, treat her as a deadly enemy?"

When enemies harm us, we should visualize them in this way. We should cease to hate them virulently and to seek revenge. We should also sincerely make this wish from our heart: May the guru and the Three Jewels bless them, and may they soon find peace, happiness, and eternal liberation from the sea of suffering!

Rejoice in the Fortune and Merit of Others

As a person who has generated Mahayana *bodhichitta*, I am the one who should bring happiness to living beings. But now that they have found wealth and fame through their own merit and virtue, how can I harbor jealousy? They are like a son who originally needed financial support from his parents but later made a lot of money through his own efforts and abilities. It really would not make sense for his parents to be jealous. Thus, when others find success in obtaining wealth, prestige, or power, we should not be envious; if we do, we have fallen under the influence of the demons.

Some people experience powerful jealousy. When they see others with more fame or wealth than themselves, they feel awful, as if their own merit and fortune had been stolen. But in reality, what others possess has nothing whatsoever to do with you. Their wealth, power, success, and prestige are all because of their own merit and fortune. No matter how envious you are, you will not share a drop of it.

At our Larung Gar Five Sciences Buddhist Academy, there really isn't envy among the three hundred or four hundred *khenpos* and *tulkus*; everyone praises one another's merit and virtue. This way, wherever they go, each receives their due prestige.

Yet some people believe that the spreading of someone else's fame will eclipse their own reputation, or that another's fall from grace will cause their own star to rise. This is undoubtedly deluded and wishful thinking.

In fact, even if everyone in the world possessed perfect merit and virtue, it still would not cause the slightest harm to your personal reputation. On the other hand, if everyone were living in poverty and hardship, you also would not gain any status from that. Therefore, when others possess fortune and merit, there is no need to be so envious. Rather, you should be full of joy and sincerely rejoice for them!

"I Am the Most Lowly Person in the Whole World"

Pride is a sense of satisfaction in your own knowledge, wealth, and so forth, and the display of it in your words or actions.

Many people do not realize that all the things they possess, including their wealth, status, and talent, are merely the fruits of good deeds cultivated in the past. If you are attached to these and become foolishly conceited, you will definitely destroy the original virtues and no longer be able to generate virtue and merit in your mind.

People who are proud always believe their wisdom to be without equal and their talent to tower over the common.

But you only need to look carefully to realize how insignificant they are. At a specific time or within a particular context, your talent or appearance or some other attribute might indeed be outstanding in some respect. But do not forget that in this world, there are countless others who surpass you tens of millions of times over.

Besides, even if your virtue and merit are incomparable among worldly people, there must be some noble beings* who surpass you. Furthermore, your supposed virtue and merit will not exist forever. They are produced merely by the gathering of causes and conditions and are extremely impermanent.

When I was a student in Sershul, I met the great spiritual masters Khenpo Chokgyur and Khenpo Peldzom. Although I did not know much about Khenpo Chokgyur, I fancied my wisdom superior to his. I did not expect that his merit and virtue and his realization would really be inconceivable. Throughout his whole life, he maintained the practice of the most profound Dharma. Even right before his death, he was still teaching the Buddhadharma to his disciples. Through study, reflection, and practicing the Dharma, he perfected his life.

As for Khenpo Peldzom, I once received his teachings on the five great Mahayana treatises and many other texts. In the past I had heard that his wisdom and character were very good; later I thought he had already aged and was perhaps

* A noble being (Skt. *arya*; Tib. *'phags pa*) is one who has attained a significant level of realization.

befuddled. But when we met two years ago, I discovered that his wisdom had only increased, yet there was not the slightest hint of pride in him. His character was still of utmost virtue, and he took great care in everything he did. I could only admire him, thinking, "A true practitioner should be just like him!"

I thought in my youth that my wisdom surpassed theirs, but in our old age, they have left me far behind. What does this illustrate? It shows that some of our merit and virtue are only temporary; there is no need to gloat over them.

In bygone years, my teacher Thupga Rinpoche had many exceedingly wise and disciplined practitioners by his side. They were as numerous as the stars. Yet in more recent times, quite a number of them had fallen into deplorable states. In contrast, those who were not so pure in maintaining the precepts or had relatively little wisdom have now become extraordinary monks and masters. When we consider these stories, we can see that even if we have wisdom, good fortune, and merit now, these are not necessarily immutable. We really should not look down on others because of them.

Until we have attained the ability to know the minds of others, there is simply no way for us to directly perceive their hidden virtue and merit. Some people's speech and actions may appear improper, but their inner virtue and merit might be as vast as the ocean. Thus, we should never belittle or act arrogantly toward anyone.

For worldly people with heavy karmic obscurations, afflictions and virtues are always mixed together, just like feces mixed into a medicine that cures all ills. What is there for us to be proud of? If you are going to take pride because of a little bit of virtue and merit, then why not feel ashamed because of your blazing afflictions?

The Venerable Dromtönpa once said, "In this whole world, I am the most lowly person." The Venerable Atisha also said, "If one is learned, one will be especially humble." These greatly accomplished masters, who possessed sublime virtues and were free of any imperfection, were humble and saw all beings as equals. As ordinary beings whose flaws are as numerous as dust motes, what right do we have to be so full of pride?

Extremely arrogant and self-righteous people tend to get shot by the demon king's flower arrow. We must never believe ourselves to be above others. Rather, we should learn to be humble and restrained, like a well-trained steed that allows anyone to ride it, and respectfully serve others.

In short, in ultimate reality, all phenomena are like empty space. There is no craving, anger, or other affliction. In conventional reality, however, illusory and dreamlike manifestations do not disappear. If we tame our minds with the pith instructions of the Great Perfection, we will understand that all phenomena have no intrinsic existence. Everything we see and hear is of great emptiness. At the same time, on the conventional level, all of samsara can still manifest, so we regard it all with the eight similes of illusion. This is the view of the great Middle Way and the Great Perfection, and it is also the sword of wisdom emanated by the bodhisattva Manjushri's great compassion.

Wielding this sword of wisdom, we can banish attachment to the self and afflictions, and we can destroy ignorance and delusion. If ignorance and delusion can be uprooted, then, like a three-legged stool that has one broken leg and cannot remain upright, the entire demon palace will collapse. From then on, no demon can do you harm!

2

The True Face of Afflictions

> SOME PEOPLE ONLY pay attention to whether
> their actions and speech are pure and only care
> about whether their external manner is appro-
> priate. But they overlook their inner intentions
> and thoughts. This is like only washing your face
> and taking a bath, but never knowing to cleanse
> the spirit.

All Miseries Begin with the Discriminating Mind

In this world, the discriminating mind has brought us infinite suffering.

Take craving, for example. When a man loves a woman
and joins with her in marriage, initially he finds her beauty
to be unparalleled. But after a time, his interest in her wanes,
and eventually he no longer finds her lovable at all. Then he
starts to pursue other women. In fact, the woman he previously adored and the wife he now detests are one and the
same. This dramatic difference between his past and present
attitudes is due entirely to the trickery of his discriminating

mind. Yet once this deluded discriminating mind exists, the person drifts like a cotton thread in the wind, seeking A today, liking B tomorrow. In the end, he will regard the beauty he eventually finds as too ordinary.

Just think—if beauty truly had a solid, unchangeable nature, then this man could not have undergone such an enormous transformation over time. Once you like someone, you would like that person forever, and the rest of the world would feel the same way you do. But this is not the way it is. One man finds a particular woman exceptionally charming and breathtaking, yet other men view her as rather unremarkable. These are the different expressions of discriminating mind.

Here is another instance: humans are universally disgusted by feces and view them as impure and filthy, yet to pigs and dogs they are a rare delicacy. All judgments of beautiful or foul, good or bad, are derived from living beings' discriminating minds at a particular moment. In truth, neither absolute good nor absolute bad exists in external objects.

The nature of everything in the world is impermanent and empty; there is no phenomenon that is worthy of our trust or reliance. However, because of the deluded discriminating mind, ordinary beings mistakenly believe that external objects truly exist, see the impure as pure, view suffering as happiness, and cling to the impermanent as permanent, and thus they fetter their own minds and act in myriad misguided ways.

For instance, so many people have paid a bitter price just to pursue a beautiful woman. But what for? The discriminating mind brings us endless misfortune and fools us into doing many utterly meaningless things. Each of us must recognize this as soon as possible and then use the wisdom of Buddhadharma to uproot it.

We need to understand that all confused discriminating thoughts are like a butcher's knife made of paper. If we recognize its true nature, this fake knife can no longer harm us. If we do not, we will continue to drift with the discriminating mind. No matter how much we possess, we will never have happiness.

Even Romantic Love Is a Form of Craving

Craving, in broad terms, means the grasping at any phenomenon in terms of form, sound, smell, taste, touch, and so forth. In a narrow sense, craving refers to romantic love and clinging between man and woman.

In traditional Tibetan parlance, craving refers to young men's and women's grasping with respect to the opposite sex. But actually, it is not only the young who have craving; even elderly people with one foot in the grave, especially those with strong habitual tendencies from the past, also experience craving that burns like an inferno. It is truly as the Tibetan proverb says, "Though old and feeble, one still favors beautiful maidens."

The mutual attraction between man and woman is a craving that is at the root of many sufferings. If you observe carefully, you will realize that whether it is the body of a man or a woman, it is all empty and impermanent; what is there to cling to? Yet it is just this demon of craving that has deluded all beings in the three realms of existence and kept them from attaining liberation. A person with craving can never come close to being reborn in Sukavati, the realm of bliss or to attaining the fruition of arhatship, let alone attaining enlightenment.

Here is an example: A man is infatuated with a woman when suddenly death approaches him. At that moment he definitely would not remember the merit of Sukavati, nor would he visualize or pray to Buddha Amitabha. Instead, he would continue to cling to the woman and would die in this state of obsessive reluctance, hastening his journey to the *bardo*. In his next life, still compelled by craving, he might very well be an insect on his lover's body.

It is said in several sutras that a woman's craving is generally stronger, but a man's craving can also be unimaginably powerful. Craving can be divided into the three levels of strong, average, and weak. Shakyamuni Buddha himself said that among his followers, Nanda's craving was particularly ingrained.

In short, anyone who cannot part from craving, whether a man or a woman, will be bound by the chains of suffering and never have a life of tranquillity.

Craving Only Grows Stronger When Indulged

Living beings' greed and desire can never be sated; the more one enjoys, the greater desire grows.

It is like someone who has never experienced sexual relations; although the person has desire, it is not yet so strong as to be out of control. But if sexual desire has been indulged once, then it is sought more and more and continues to grow, never to be fulfilled.

Some people naïvely believe that they will be fulfilled after experiencing the pleasure of passion just once. But it is undoubtedly wild fancy to believe that through this alone their desire can be abated. It is akin to drinking salty water: the more you drink, the thirstier you become. Craving and desire are only further enflamed the more you indulge them, never allowing you to willingly let go.

Think about it: If craving really did abate after satisfaction, then the many people who have been satisfied innumerable times in their lives should no longer experience it. Yet our craving has continued to grow instead of lessening over time. Why?

In truth, the pleasure of sex is the most seductive desire in the world. Even after wallowing in it for a lifetime, people do not feel satisfied. The happiness that craving brings us is scant and short-lived, but its bitter fruits must be borne by us for many lifetimes.

A beast of burden must endure endless beatings just to eat a handful of grass by the side of the road. It may get as little as one mouthful of grass, yet its body and mind have suffered tremendous pain. Little gain, much pain—worldly craving and desire are just this.

Since craving harms us so greatly, you cannot hope to weaken it by satisfying it; if you wish to truly eradicate it, you need to rely on the pith instructions of Buddhadharma as antidotes.

An Angry Person Does Not Have the Slightest Chance to Be Happy

If we harbor anger, we can never be free. We will not even have any hope of finding happiness or the respect of others. In fact, anger is an inferno that consumes our mind. In a single moment, it can completely destroy all of our roots of virtue. In this world, there is no fault more grave than anger.

If we wish to eradicate anger, we must do everything possible to cultivate the practice of equality between others and ourselves. We need to understand that just as we prefer happiness, so do others; just as we do not wish to suffer, neither do they. By extrapolating from our own experience, we will know that when others hurt us, they are also helpless and bound by afflictions. Understanding this, we will no longer quibble over trivial matters and can even wish them peace and happiness.

If this compassionate mind that sees the equality of oneself and others can manifest often in a person's inner thoughts and outer actions, and can be generated toward any being, then this person is like a wish-fulfilling jewel that nourishes and benefits all beings. Not only this, she will also be filled with joy, her wishes will naturally be fulfilled, everything in her present and future will go smoothly, and her merit will grow daily like the waxing moon and never dwindle.

Without a shadow of doubt, this kind of person is everything that is dignified in the world.

The Greater the Delusion, the Darker the Path Ahead

Once ignorance and delusion are present, they are bound to obstruct our temporary and long-term happiness. Why? From ignorance is born affliction; afflictions can then lead us to commit evil actions; and evil actions then bring on all manner of suffering. From this you can see that ignorance is the source of affliction and suffering and the root of all faults.

Hidden within every being is a great demon king. This is none other than ignorance and delusion.

Not understanding the effects of good or evil actions; not studying, reflecting on, and practicing the Dharma—this is a kind of delusion. Not having any understanding of emptiness that is free from conceptual elaboration—this too is a kind of delusion. Not having a shred of comprehension of the dependent origination of infallible cause and effect—this is a kind of delusion as well. Therefore, what we need to eliminate now is this delusion of not understanding the effects of actions; what we need to uproot ultimately is the ignorance of not thoroughly realizing the nature of all phenomena.

When ignorance and delusion are concealed within a person, it is as if he has been bewitched by an evil spell. His future will only become darker and darker. What methods can we use to dispel ignorance and delusion? There is only one answer: the teachings of the most compassionate and loving Shakyamuni Buddha.

In this world, only the Buddha has cut through all ignorance and delusion. Although bodhisattvas like Maitreya and

Manjushri have attained extremely high states of realization, they must also rely on the Buddha's teachings when they transform and liberate sentient beings.

For instance, the bodhisattva Maitreya, who abides on the tenth bodhisattva level, is the future fifth buddha of this fortunate aeon. The content of his work *Ornament of Clear Realization* still relies on Shakyamuni Buddha's *Prajnaparamita Sutra:* some of it is based on the *Mahaprajnaparamita Sutra,* some on the *Medium Prajnaparamita Sutra,* and some on the *Verse Summary of Prajnaparamita.* If we study and read further in the Tripitaka, we will find that every verse in the *Ornament of Clear Realization* can be traced to its source in the Buddha's sutras. Numerous teachings in the *Ornament of Clear Realization* also specifically mention how the bodhisattva Maitreya relied on the sutras to reveal the Buddha's profound and hidden meanings. Similarly, when many bodhisattvas of the first level and above (like the bodhisattva Nagarjuna) teach the Buddhadharma, they also rely on Buddha's teachings.

Yet some ordinary beings today who have only a minimal understanding of Buddhism believe they know it all. They are arrogant and readily question the Buddha's views. This deluded action is really to be pitied. In order to develop our wisdom, it is perfectly reasonable for us to examine and analyze the Buddha's teaching carefully. But to try to refute it is to indulge in the wildest fancy.

At present, there is an endless stream of all sorts of mistaken teachings. I hope that whenever anyone teaches the Buddhadharma, they do not depart from the Buddha's teachings, and certainly do not interpret Buddhadharma by following their own discriminating mind. Otherwise, whether they are composing commentaries and books or teaching others the Dharma, all their activities will merely work in concert with ignorance and delusion and cannot possibly become their antidotes!

Craving, Anger, and Delusion Are the Root of All Misery

I hope that everyone, whether lay or monastic, will lead a lifestyle that is not perverted. What is included in a perverted lifestyle? For example, not studying, reflecting, or practicing the Dharma with diligence, and frequently violating precepts and breaking one's vows. Or, unwilling to study the Dharma seriously, instead going here and there to beg for alms and pursuing self-interested gain, or returning to one's hometown and assisting family members in worldly pursuits. These all belong to a perverted lifestyle.

Our every suffering and happiness is in reality created by our own karma. Particularly, the root of suffering is none other than the three poisons of craving, anger, and delusion. The bodhisattva Nagarjuna said, "Craving, anger, delusion, and the karma born of these are all unwholesome; the absence of craving, anger, delusion, and the karma born of these are all wholesome."

You must know that in our daily speech, actions, and thoughts, whatever is tainted by craving, anger, and delusion is all unwholesome karma. Only that which has cut off craving, anger, and delusion is virtuous Dharma. Thus, seeking all means to banish craving, anger, and delusion is vitally important to all of us. Only when we are free from these poisons can we ever attain ultimate, deep-rooted happiness and peace!

3

Suffering and Happiness
Are Both Impermanent

BECAUSE WE HAVE been born as human beings, we should pursue a spiritual path. If we do not, we will have squandered this precious human body. That would be like arriving at a treasure island brimming with gold but leaving empty-handed without taking any treasure. What a pitiful waste that would be!

We Often Ask for Our Own Bitter Pills

The sublime teaching of Buddhadharma is like a divine nectar that heals all ills. When those who have the propensity listen to it and put it into practice, they can purify their afflictions of craving, anger, and delusion.

Each person experiences different phenomena as the result of past karma, and thus the suffering and happiness that arise from our individual karma are also as far apart as heaven and earth. Even among a family of three who live in the same house and always eat together, each person's experiences will be markedly different: one might have auspicious dreams at night and enjoy good health, while another might suffer from endless nightmares, physical discomfort, and mental unease. No matter who they are or how intimately they are related, no two people can possibly share the same experience.

Where do these myriad and strange experiences of suffering and happiness ultimately come from? They are not caused by external objects; they originate from our mind.

If our mind is filled with compassion and confidence, then we are sure to be happy and peaceful in this life. If we also imbue our mind with immaculate wisdom, we will even attain perfect ultimate liberation. But if we often generate unwholesome thoughts and create negative karma, then what undoubtedly await us are the ferocious lower realms and intolerable pain and suffering.

Shakyamuni Buddha also pointed out in the sutras, "Mind is the source of all phenomena. Thus it is called the all-creating king." Why is it said to be "all-creating"? It is because the mind can create pure nirvana, and it can also create impure samsara. That is to say, all phenomena in samsara are manifestations of the impure mind; nirvana and wisdom are manifestations of the pure mind.

If we observe further, we will discover that we cannot find anything substantial in external objects. Thus, the sole root of purity and impurity is our own mind. Since the mind can manifest all phenomena within samsara and nirvana, then if we turn our mind toward the virtuous Dharma, peace and happiness are within sight. If we cannot tame our mind, and often commit unwholesome and harmful deeds under the power of the afflictions, then we are surely asking for our own bitter pills in the future.

Where Will You Go after Your Death?

Some people with power and wealth live in pleasant environs, surrounded by many who sing their praises. But even so, they too will one day face the terrifying grim reaper just like everyone else. They will not have any freedom. Indeed, there are quite a few who exhaust their fortune and merit during their lifetime; they end up bankrupt, experiencing the myriad wiles of impermanence.

Thus, human suffering and happiness are not certain. They are like the grains of rice that rise and sink in the pot when boiled. At times we feel happiness due to wholesome karma, and at other times we experience enormous suffering because of unwholesome karma. Happiness and suffering forever shadow us; as one rises, the other falls.

Take myself as an example: Since I was a child, I have followed wise spiritual mentors in practicing the Buddhadharma. Thus I could be seen as someone who has fortune and virtue. On the other hand, since I was a child my health has always been poor; I am frequently dogged by illness. I have also encountered such hardships as having nothing to eat or wear. Although I believe that my practice is not too bad, and I have also undertaken many barely tolerable ascetic practices, I still cannot be certain when I ask myself, "Where will I go after death?"

Today, getting enough food and clothing is no longer an issue for me; I have already received all the fame and fortune I am due, and my students all respect me. I should feel peaceful and happy. Yet viewed from a different angle, I am also a very pitiful old man. My limbs are so unwieldy that I cannot even walk to the Dharma hall without help. I experience hardly a moment of physical well-being all day long. One or two years ago, as I reflected that Mipham Rinpoche suffered from severe illness starting at the age of fifty and died at sixty-seven, I aspired to die at sixty-seven too and be reborn in a pure land. Later, however, due to various causes and conditions, my life was somewhat prolonged.

Hence, using me as an example, everyone should examine closely and reflect on this: What happiness and suffering have you experienced in your life? If you wish to be often happy and no longer suffer in the future, then what should you do? Perhaps you have never before considered these questions about your future. But from this moment, you can try to quiet your mind and ponder them.

When You Leave This Life Behind, Your Virtue Is Your Sole Defense

Mipham Rinpoche once said, "Samsara's peace and happiness are as fleeting as lightning, not dependable in the slightest."

Now that you have the precious human body and have also listened to the sublime Buddhadharma, no matter who you are, right now, you should take good advantage of this opportunity to practice. Only then can you face death with confidence. Just as Patrul Rinpoche said, "Cast aside rebirth once and for all!" If you practice diligently, then after you cast aside your human body at the end of this life, you will never again cycle in samsara due to your karma and afflictions, and you will be eternally liberated from the ocean of suffering.

But what is truly regrettable is that many people always believe themselves to be very far from death. They never ponder death; they spend their whole lives zealously pursuing fame and fortune, completely unconcerned with liberation. They lead a decadent life, not knowing that impermanence can arrive at any moment and the extreme terror of death can strike them down in an instant.

In reality, no one can predict when or where the grim reaper will appear. When that day arrives, even if our closest family and friends surround us, shriek our name until they're hoarse, rend their hearts and lungs with their cries, and even faint from their great sorrow, death will not show mercy. At that moment, no matter how attached and unwilling, we must still part from this world and walk all alone on the desolate path of the *bardo*.

It is just as described in *The Way of the Bodhisattva:*

> There I'll be, prostrate upon my bed,
> And all around, my family and friends.

But I alone shall be the one to feel
The cutting of the thread of life.
And when the heralds of the Deadly King have
    gripped me,
What help to me will be my friends and kin?
For then life's virtue is my one defense,
And this, alas, is what I shrugged away.*

In the not-so-distant future, we are all destined to walk this path, departing from this illusory, impermanent world and from our most cherished friends and family. Thus, we do not need to be overly attached to everything in this life. Rather, we should hurry and practice the authentic Dharma for long-lasting peace and happiness, and make ample preparation for the arrival of death.

There Is No Need to Cling to the Past

Nothing in this world is immutable and changeless. Take the body. When young, your face is like a white water lily tinged with red, so handsome and lovely. Even if you are exquisitely beautiful, when you age and grow sallow, you too will be like a shriveled stump of rotten wood. By then, even you will be repulsed when you see yourself. You can only silently yearn for your long-lost youth, which will never return.

* Shantideva, *The Way of the Bodhisattva: A Translation of the Bodhicharyā-vatāra* (revised edition), translated by the Padmakara Translation Group (Boston: Shambhala Publications, 2006), 2:40-41.

How many people are willing to admire an aged body? We elderly people in our sixties find that young people recoil at the sight of us. But one can foresee that in the not-so-distant future, their own handsome, tall, straight bodies will surely deteriorate like ours.

No matter where or when, there has never been an exceptional individual for whom birth, aging, illness, and death do not exist. Even Chakravartin and Indra both displayed impermanence in the end. How could these frail, fleshly bodies of ours not wane and decay day by day?

Not only is the body impermanent, but there is nothing in the external world that is not similarly subject to change. High mountains and flat plains, cities and villages, the vast Gobi Desert—locales of every form and color have parts that please the eye and mind and also parts that are dangerous and threatening. But they will all ultimately be destroyed by impermanence and undergo complete transformation, just as the sea can be transformed into mulberry fields.

Since there is nothing in the external world or within ourselves that is constant and unchanging, what need is there to cling to what we now possess?

Although each person's happiness and suffering is different, we have one thing in common: our happiness and suffering are like a flash of lightning in the sky. They are all impermanent. Yet many people do not realize this. They grasp at illusory and insubstantial things like the body, like wealth, and for the sake of these things they create all kinds of unwholesome karma. It is only when they face death that they suddenly realize that despite everything they have striven for, they cannot take with them even a strand of hair. Instead, it is only the wholesome and unwholesome karma they created in this life that will follow them—pursuing them like a shadow.

Do Not Think That Youth Is Indestructible

Young people may be perfect in their looks, talent, or fortune, but there is no need to be proud of these things. You may compare well with many people around you, but in this world there must be some you do not know who can outshine you.

When you are young, you should have a humble heart and be fully aware of impermanence. Do not think that any phenomenon is constant or unchanging. In my life, I have witnessed many people of prominence fall to pitiful positions in the end. A wealthy person suddenly becomes poverty-stricken; a poor person turns wealthy in the blink of an eye. Everything on this earth undergoes similar drastic changes.

The impermanence of wealth is like a cloud floating in the sky. The impermanence of status is like mist shrouding a mountaintop. The impermanence of good reputation is like an echo in an empty valley. When others envy your looks, talent, wisdom, and so forth, please remember that this is like being praised in a dream and has little substance or meaning!

These things are quite important to worldly people, but when we are dying, there is nothing in the world that we can bring along with us; everything must definitely be left behind. Hence, it is best if we do not crave and tightly cling to worldly concerns like reputation, wealth, and status. Otherwise, we will only experience endless suffering.

If There Is No Stain on Your Face, There Is No Stain in the Mirror

All of the suffering we experience is the fruition of unwholesome actions we committed in the past. Many people, however, have not truly recognized this. As a result, when they encounter the slightest difficulty, they either blame their friends and family for being incapable or complain that life has not given them sufficient opportunities. They do not know that the root of suffering and happiness is the self. This is truly the height of folly.

To give an analogy, if there is no stain on our face, then a mirror will not reflect it. Similarly, if we had never committed unwholesome karma in this life or in a previous lifetime, we could never inexplicably attract suffering.

When I was severely ill, a number of people thought it was a disturbance caused by demon beings or due to impure donations offered by some lay practitioners. But I knew clearly that it was the result of my past karma.

In fact, I am not alone in this. Every living being's sufferings are all related to their past karma. On the surface, it appears that external objects have a direct bearing on our happiness and suffering, but in reality, they are only operating under the power of karma. The people who hurt you are also controlled by karma and have no command over themselves.

The moment karma ripens, then no matter how much money or power we have, we lack any means to eliminate the bitter fruits we once sowed. Even if we had the miraculous powers of a god or goddess, they would be of no avail in the face of karma. If we wish to completely purify our karma, this is possible only by confessing our wrongdoings!

4

Buddha Mind

THE HEART OF Buddhadharma is the cultivation of compassion and loving-kindness. Loving-kindness is the wish for all beings to attain peace and happiness; compassion is the wish for all beings to be free from suffering. No matter who you are, you should develop these qualities that bring benefit to yourself and others.

Be Compassionate toward Everyone

Regardless of where or when, as it becomes our habit to treat everyone with compassion and loving-kindness, even enemies who initially wanted to obstruct us will gradually grow fond of us. If we can see all people, great or small, as equals and treat them with wholehearted compassion and loving-kindness, then they will overlook whatever flaws we may have and will delight in spreading our good name.

If we wish for others to help us, then we must first offer to help them. As more and more people become truly fond of us, the opposing forces in our lives will gradually diminish. Even if some people were not initially in agreement with us, our virtuous intentions will move them to speak well of us.

In contrast, should you create enemies everywhere and incite them to voice their grievances, it will be difficult for you to succeed at anything you do. If you wish to be accepted by many, the most powerful Dharma jewels are compassion and loving-kindness.

Take our Buddhist academy, for example. At its inception there were only a few of us. Over time, I treated many people with compassion and loving-kindness and lived in harmony with them. Later, there were over twenty, then one hundred, then one thousand—and today there are about eight thousand people here.

Although I myself do not possess any virtue, many people now know and respect me. What are the reasons for this? It is just because I highly valued the khenpos of the Buddhist academy and often spoke in pleasant, loving words. This led them to be happy and grateful, and so they have praised me widely in public.

When some people are praised by others, deep down they really wish to conceal their virtues. But if others, especially those closely connected with you, sincerely respect you and hold you in affection, then they are sure to sing your praises wherever they go. In this way, through word of mouth, your virtues will be known far and wide.

So if you wish to win others' favor, you must first possess virtue and treat everyone with compassion and loving-kindness. You cannot belittle people as you please.

Those Who Deceive Others Are Quick to Fail

Some people always adopt a deceitful attitude in their speech or actions in daily life, whether intentionally or not. When this becomes a habit, others view everything they do as dishonest. They may find some success in the short term, but they will definitely lose out in the long run.

These people are like water flowing from a mountaintop, which starts up high but gradually descends lower and lower and cannot rise again. Accomplishing one's endeavors through deceit is both dishonest and unreliable. In the end, one will not gain any long-term benefits.

In comparison, some people's actions are honest and just, and they meet everything with compassion and loving-kindness. If someone harms them out of jealousy, they experience fleeting irritation. Ultimately, not only will they not fail, but they will find increasing success.

People who like to play clever tricks may seem shrewd, but they are actually rather foolish. They are focused only on small immediate gains and never consider that their actions will often accomplish the very opposite of what they seek. In contrast, people with great wisdom and capabilities tend to see farther and deeper; they always plan for the long term. These people are bound to realize limitless happiness and peace in their present and future lives.

Do Not Wish to Lean on the Powerful

There are people of low status who particularly adore wealthy and powerful bigwigs. They act extremely deferential, hovering around them, nodding and bowing—fawning over them like sycophants. But actually, it is not very meaningful to serve these high and mighty people. When it comes to worldly benefits, they will not give you much. As for character, wisdom, and the cultivation of transcendental teachings, it is even less likely that they will be of any help at all.

It is just like an old man who, burning with desire, vainly pursues a beautiful young maiden. Not only will the maiden be displeased, she might even glare furiously at him. Similarly, those in humble positions cannot possibly attain their desires by placing their hopes in so-called privileged people.

Then there are people who have an endless flow of desires. They are always waiting for unrealistic things to happen. Spending their days and nights in worry, they make happiness and peace rare in their lives. They do not know how much longer they will live, yet they are always planning to make a big impact here or accomplish an important project there. Every day thinking wishfully like this, they really are to be pitied.

In brief, all these actions are in conflict with the Dharma. If you calm your mind and reflect, you will discover that not only are they of no true benefit to you, but they also hasten the vain passing of life.

Those Who Are Ungrateful
Will Not Enjoy Any Virtue or Merit

If others helped me when I was impoverished or in pain, then later, when my wealth and influence were more satisfactory, I did not forget them. To do otherwise would make me a contemptible, lowly character, no matter how high my reputation or status.

Nowadays some people are like this: As soon as they gain a little status, they erase any memory of their past benefactors. They abandon those who showed them kindness and take up with someone who is more influential, and then later they repeat the cycle again. It is utterly pointless to associate with such people.

When making friends, the key is to see their character. Friends of good character—even though they may not be particularly close to you and may even think ill of you in some ways—would never do anything to harm you. But if people are willing to abandon their old friends just to befriend you, then they are unreliable and will one day treat you the same way.

There are even those who treat their teacher this way. When they meet a more renowned teacher, they discard their original teacher. Such ungrateful people are not very grounded at all.

A long time ago, three lamas traveled from afar to seek the Dharma from Do Khyentse Yeshe Dorje Rinpoche. Rinpoche said to them, "If you abandon all of your former teachers, I will teach you."

At the time, two of the lamas felt that their former teachers were of little fame, whereas Khyentse Rinpoche's reputation spread far and wide, so they agreed. But the remaining lama thought, "Khyentse Rinpoche may be an extraordinary master, but my former teacher has been profoundly kind to me. I would rather forgo this chance to seek the Dharma than abandon my teacher."

Seeing this, Khyentse Rinpoche said to the first two lamas, "If you treat your former teachers in this manner, you will surely treat me the same way in the future. You two are not worthy Dharma vessels, so you cannot receive my teachings. The other lama can stay."

Later, that lama received a great many Dharma teachings from Rinpoche and attained sublime states of realization. His name is Lama Ösel.

The More Wealth and Power You Have, the More You Should Esteem Those around You

As your status increases, you need to have ever greater compassion and loving-kindness for everyone below you. At the same time, do not grovel before the people above you. Be neither haughty nor overly humble.

In ancient Tibet, great rulers and Dharma kings such as Songtsen Gampo, Trisong Detsen, and Tri Ralpachen all conducted state affairs through the Buddhadharma. Despite their superior position, they always acted with compassion and loving-kindness toward all beings, especially the wretched.

Some people, as soon as they gain a little status, start to speak and act harshly to those beneath them. Yet they fawn over their superiors, nodding their heads and wagging their tails, hoping to receive more esteem and money in return. Then there are those who have attained high status but not brought themselves or others much benefit. For instance, there are some eminent monks and masters who have not contributed anything to the lives of beings or to the Buddhadharma. These people are like ornaments in the dark—unseen by all.

In addition, as a person of power and influence, you should be discerning in meting out rewards and punishments. Those who have acted well should be duly rewarded. For instance, during the time of King Gesar, only people with a strong wish to benefit others would be chosen as ministers.

In short, live in harmony with everyone, have compassion and loving-kindness, respect superiors, care for subordinates, and do not chase after fame and fortune. A person of this ilk can be a leader.

To Profit at Another's Expense Is to Act Contrary to Cause and Effect

As a high-level manager, whether you are a Dharma teacher or a senior official, you must possess both worldly and transcendent wisdom. Stand high and see far, be skilled at acting in accordance with the principle of cause and effect, and be unbiased when resolving issues. In particular, when you handle property and wealth, you must never misappropriate them.

To profit at others' expense is to act contrary to cause and effect. Even if your walk is ordinarily upright and your disposition naturally compassionate and kind, if you do not place great importance on cause and effect, you will only cause your own ruin in the end.

After all, financial loss is only a temporary suffering; loss of reputation is a single-lifetime suffering; but harmful actions that do not accord with the principle of cause and effect will create suffering in life after life. Therefore, it does not matter if you do not possess wealth or fame, but you must never lose the correct view on cause and effect.

The foolish always obsess over minute, short-term gains, but the wise plan for the long term. Only the pursuit of perfecting one's merit and virtue is the cause of all happiness and perfection. So no matter who you are, it is best not to cling to wealth. Instead, reflect often on impermanence and cautiously choose actions according to the principle of cause and effect. Only this can lead you to greater peace and happiness!

If You Love False Speech, Beware of Retribution

Nowadays, people often claim that when they were in such-and-such a meditative state, they saw their guru or the Buddha or their meditation deities and so on. You need to see such people's true colors clearly and never just stand there and let their tongues run away with them. At the same time, I hope people like this who spread falsehoods are attentive to the retribution of cause and effect.

When the First Döndrup Rinpoche resided in Larung, there was a local practitioner by the name of Akhyong Senge. Sometimes he placed a hat on his head and claimed he had developed the *ushnisha.** At other times he alleged he could fly. When he really did leap from a high rooftop, however, he was severely injured.

One time, he claimed to be in possession of many *termas*** and demanded that Döndrup Rinpoche authenticate them. After seeing the termas, Döndrup Rinpoche said honestly, "These are not true termas; you may have fallen under the power of Mara."

But Akhyong Senge did not believe this. Not only did he insist that his "termas" were genuine; he also slandered Döndrup Rinpoche, claiming that he had said what he did out of envy. Later, he found another highly accomplished master to vouch for the authenticity of these supposed termas. Still they were not accepted.

However, he stubbornly held on to his view, and finally he went before Jamyang Khyentse Rinpoche to demand authentication. Rinpoche skillfully signed for the false termas and also asked him to chant the Padmasambhava heart mantra ten million times, saying that only then could the result of the authentication be revealed.

After Akhyong Senge completed his recitation of the mantra according to the requirement, in his meditative state he

---

* Ushnisha (Skt.): The protuberance on the crown of a buddha's head.
** Terma (Tib.): Literally, "hidden treasure"; texts by Padmasambhava that were hidden in rocks, caves, and other locations to be discovered and propagated by later masters.

suddenly saw a monk fall to the ground, and his self-righteous illusion was shattered. At that point he awoke and began to transform in the direction of a true practitioner.

Actually, Akhyong Senge was indeed under the power of Mara at the time. Later, through the power of the mantra and Jamyang Khyentse Rinpoche's sublime blessings, he was able to dispel this adversity and return to normal.

We can learn from the example of Akhyong Senge. The realms of awareness perceived by worldly people are not necessarily true or reliable. The reason some can see images of buddhas and bodhisattvas day and night is but the external manifestation of their bodies' channels, energies, and essences. They are nothing to delight in or boast about.

If you encounter such a situation in the future, remember that you must never boast to others that you have directly seen buddhas and bodhisattvas. This amounts to major lies, thoroughly and completely!

Fondness for Bustling Gatherings Leads to Immense Faults

Throughout history, worldly people have always tended to resist loneliness. They take delight in distractions and are fond of spending time in lively, bustling places. At the mere rustle of leaves in the wind, people rush to gather and set their tongues wagging animatedly. If some dispute occurs nearby, people become even more excited—the so-called honest and rule-abiding ones stay out of it and watch from the sidelines, while the busybodies add fuel to the fire with their gossip and chatter.

In his *Letter to a Friend,* the bodhisattva Nagarjuna described the faults of partaking in busy gatherings. In *Advice from Me to Myself,* Patrul Rinpoche also taught that we should generally remain in one place. He also told us to let the body calmly abide in the room and let the mind calmly abide in the body.

Yet people nowadays cannot stay away from crowds or remain for long in one place. Even in everyday conversations, voices are becoming louder and louder. Actually, whoever who you are, in daily life you should be peaceful in mind and be gentle and leisurely in speech, not scream and shout at will.

As for not preferring distractions, perhaps some will ask, "There are so many monks and nuns in your Buddhist academy. Is this not a form of distraction?" Those who question in this way are clearly not aware that the internal source of distraction is the mind. A greater or lesser number of people is not the root cause of distraction. If your mind is easily drawn to and tainted by external objects, then even if you lived alone on a remote mountain, such problems would still occur.

Whether Rich or Poor, Have an Altruistic Mind

Some eminent monks and masters are afraid of being burdened by fame, so they choose not to cling to personal possessions and often adopt the appearance of ascetic practitioners in order to guide living beings. But there are also highly accomplished masters who, in order to benefit more beings, are obliged to be "tainted" by worldly fame and gain.

Patrul Rinpoche and Kongtrul Yönten Gyatso were both renowned adepts during their time, and they were also intimate friends. Kongtrul Rinpoche had many disciples in Sershul, and in his daily life, he was like the moon surrounded by a myriad of stars. Even his horses and possessions were too numerous to count.

One time when the two were together, Patrul Rinpoche grew tired of Kongtrul Rinpoche's fame and accumulated wealth, so he said to those beside him, "Kongtrul Yönten Gyatso now enjoys widespread renown and abundant wealth. For an ascetic monk like me to remain here would greatly spoil the scene, I fear. It is better that I leave."

When Kongtrul Rinpoche heard this, he begged repeatedly for him to stay. Patrul Rinpoche said jokingly, "Back when we listened to the Buddhadharma at the feet of Gyurme Thutob Namgyal in Shechen, not only were our clothes threadbare, but our house was also simple and crude, and we were frequently bullied by others. To fill our stomachs, we often went begging for alms together. Do you remember that? Now you have become a famous high monk and no longer need me to do anything for you. What point is there in my staying here?"

Upon hearing this, Kongtrul Rinpoche shook his head and said, "Please do not think that way. I am compelled to do some things against my will, but I am definitely not coveting personal gain. If it weren't for the fact that it may benefit living beings. . . ." Hearing his dear friend's explanation, Patrul Rinpoche nodded his head in understanding.

Consider these two great masters who surpassed the ancients and amazed their contemporaries. One took the form of an ascetic monk to guide living beings to liberation, and the other the appearance of an affluent monk to benefit beings. But regardless of how they appeared, they were both selfless and served wholeheartedly to benefit living beings. In contrast, some people think of only themselves deep down, and they covet fame and fortune by hook or by crook. How is this worthy of reverence by anyone?

Do Not Grumble about External Circumstances

When harmed by enemies, those with little wisdom naturally respond with anger and cannot help adopting all kinds of revenge tactics. One can easily imagine the result.

Shakyamuni Buddha emphasized that all suffering and happiness originate from our own past karma. If we place the blame for our suffering on external factors and other people instead of assiduously confessing our karmic obscurations, then boundless afflictions will only grow. It is just like people suffering from gallstones: If they indulge in greasy foods and their condition consequently worsens, they have only themselves to blame. They should not get angry at their food.

Being angry at external circumstances can only ruin your present and future lives. Thus, even when you are ill, do not be angry at your illness; you will only heap suffering upon suffering.

The root of all misery is none other than our own mind, or one could say it is the unwholesome karma we created in the past. If we thoroughly understand this, then when misfortune strikes, we will know that we are merely reaping the fruits of our own actions. Then we will not pointlessly grumble about external circumstances.

If we inquire further, we will discover that all suffering actually originates from attachment to the self. Only when we fundamentally uproot this attachment can suffering be dispelled. It is truly as the bodhisattva Shantideva said:

> All the harm with which this world is rife,
> All the fear and suffering there is,
> Clinging to the "I" has caused it!
> What is the use of preserving this great demon?*

---

* Shantideva, *The Way of the Bodhisattva: A Translation of the Bodhicharyā-vatāra* (revised edition), translated by the Padmakara Translation Group (Boston: Shambhala Publications, 2006), 8:134.

5

It's Never Too Late

SCIENCE AND TECHNOLOGY can satisfy people's material needs and raise their standard of living. Buddhism, on the other hand, brings spiritual peace and happiness and dispels the darkness and delusion of the inner world. Without Buddhism, if we just blindly pursue material pleasures, we will only attain the very opposite of what we seek.

Do Not Let the Mind Run Wild

Every suffering in life is in fact produced by our own untamed mind. The discriminating thoughts within us are like a baby monkey that swings and jumps around. If we wish to catch it, we must use the rope of mindfulness. Otherwise, it will not remain calm or stay still for even a moment.

If we are not willing to find an antidote for the discriminating mind, its powers can be terrifying. It is like living with a bad-tempered spouse who argues all the time—the family lives with constant unease. In the same way, if there are afflictions in the mind, we will never find any peace or happiness. Not only could a bad spouse squander all of the family's resources, the other spouse might even lose his or her life. If our mental afflictions remain untamed, the result will be even more horrific than if we lived with a bad spouse.

Many people wish to be healthy, to be free from disease, and to remain forever young, but these are not very meaningful goals. If you can tame your mind, the value of this will far surpass anything in the world. Patrul Rinpoche said, "Tame the mind, tame the mind, use bodhichitta to tame the mind. Even if we do not cultivate any good deeds in body and speech, taming our mind in fact benefits ourselves and all beings."

For an ordinary person, discriminative thoughts of not wishing to suffer and fiercely clinging to comforts and delights are continually bubbling up. Yet as practitioners, we should banish this mind-set and transform all suffering and happiness into the practice. For instance, when we are suffering, it is best that we abide in emptiness. If we have not yet reached this state of realization, we practice the bodhichitta of exchanging self and other (*tonglen*), in which we visualize that we are taking on the suffering of all living beings. To practice in this way just once can accumulate merit for tens of thousands of aeons. Suffering is transformed into merit in an instant.

The Secret of Letting Go of Restlessness

Everyone has wishes and goals, but after one wish has been fulfilled, more goals follow right behind, and even greater comfort and delight are sought.

For instance, when the monks' Dharma hall at our Buddhist academy has been built, we want to build a great hall next. After the great hall is completed, we plan to rebuild the nuns' Dharma hall, and following that we want to build the mandala of Guhyagarbha. As long as I live, I will never be satisfied, because these structures will greatly benefit everyone's study and practice.

The discriminating mind is just like that: after one wish has been satisfied, a new project arises. It is like the way some people, when they have a house, wish for a courtyard; when there is a courtyard, they also need a garden. Until attachment to the self is completely eradicated, this kind of thinking will never end. Master Gendun Chopel said, "All living beings, even the smallest ants, are all rushing about for their own happiness and gain."

Whether seeking to do good deeds or pursuing meaningless activities, ultimately, we should always observe the essence of the mind, banish all discriminative thoughts of expectation and doubt, and calmly abide in the state free of clinging. Only then will afflictions disperse.

If initially the mind cannot rest calmly, you can place a statue of Shakyamuni Buddha in front of you and focus on the Buddha's heart center. If mental dullness occurs after a while, you can look upward at the ushnisha on the Buddha's head. Visualizing and meditating like this can easily tame the restless mind, and all discriminating thoughts will disappear.

When I was studying at Sershul, one day my teacher Thupga Rinpoche said, "If we do not tame the mind, the mind's powers can be incredibly fierce and terrifying. But if we try to tame it, we will discover that it is but a paper tiger. Even if we only spend a mere seven days to fervently pray to our teacher and sincerely tame our mind, the state of our mind will be vastly different from before."

I trust my teacher's words without a shadow of a doubt. In fact, as long as we are willing to make the effort and rely on the sublime practice instructions, taming the mind is not so difficult. The only reason we have never been able to achieve this is that we have not applied ourselves to it.

We Need to "Crave" Buddhas and Bodhisattvas

The Buddha once said that even to gaze at a buddha image with a distracted mind can lead to freedom from suffering and the attainment of happiness in the future. What's more, it is beneficial even to gaze at a buddha image in anger. This will lead to a brief fall to the lower realms, but because an affinity with the Buddha has been formed, eventually one will gradually awaken.

The merit of the buddha image is immense. It is said in *Letter to a Friend* that any buddha statue, regardless of its material or how finely it was crafted, even if it is molded from mud or carved from wood, is something one should respect.

Shakyamuni Buddha himself promised, "After my parinirvana, if people build buddha statues, feel gratitude or confidence toward them, and often bring them to mind, this will not be much different from if the Buddha were alive."

Thus, visualizing and meditating on a buddha statue that bears the major and minor marks of buddhahood is of great significance to our present and future lives. (Of course, visualizing and practicing the Buddha's wisdom body is of even more sublime merit.)

Consider this analogy: after a man with extremely strong craving met a peerless beauty, her dimpled smile would constantly arise in his mind. Similarly, if we also have such "craving" toward all buddhas and bodhisattvas and think of them day and night, the buddhas and bodhisattvas will never be far from us until we have attained the fruit of awakening. They will continually bless us through great compassion and bring us the accomplishment of all happiness.

You need to know that regardless of which noble being you pray to, your wisdom will grow as a result. In particular, if you wish for blessings, you should pray to your teacher; if you wish for spiritual accomplishments, you should pray to your meditation deity; to have success in your endeavors, you should pray to the *dakinis*; to dispel adversity, you should pray to the Dharma protectors. Therefore, I hope everyone can often pray in this way in order to accomplish diverse benefits.

Chanting the Name of Amitabha a Million Times, One Can Be Reborn in Sukhavati

Ideally, you should review your life from time to time, asking, "How many unwholesome actions have I committed? How much hardship have I endured?" As soon as you inquire a little, you will realize that suffering has never been far from you. So if you wish to no longer experience such unbearable suffering, you must practice diligently.

Practicing the Buddhadharma is actually not as unattainable as some believe. For example, even the most humble person can be reborn in Sukhavati. This is quite simple, right? As long as we have strong confidence in Buddha Amitabha, aspire from the core of our being to be reborn in his pure realm, follow the instructions of the teachings, and never commit the five crimes with immediate retribution or the harmful act of rejecting the Dharma, then it will be as Shakyamuni Buddha and Buddha Amitabha promised: after death, we definitely can be reborn in the blissful realm.

There was a lama who declared publicly, "Khenpo Serthar [His Holiness Jigme Phuntsok himself] said chanting the name of Amitabha one million times enables one to be reborn in the realm of Sukhavati. This is a complete lie. How could it be so easy to be reborn there?"

Perhaps this person was not very familiar with the teachings. What I said was in fact in accordance with the *Amitabha Sutra,* not a fabrication of the discriminating mind. The instruction on chanting the name one million times was unequivocally taught by my root teacher Thupga Rinpoche, His Holiness the Fourteenth Dalai Lama, and Tulku Dongak Tenpe Nyima: "In the future, if you lead those with the necessary karma and good fortune to chant one million times the name of Buddha Amitabha (here it refers to the name of Buddha Amitabha in Tibetan; the Chinese "Namo Amitabha" needs to be chanted six million times), they will be able to attain rebirth in Sukhavati."

No matter how despicable my own character, I would

never use this teaching to deceive the world. Thus, with the words of the Buddha and my teachers as testimony, I wish for everyone to sincerely aspire to chant the name of Amitabha, to choose without the least hesitation what is of the most benefit to our present and future lives, and to treasure each present moment!

Chanting the Aspiration of Bodhisattva Samantabhadra Just Once Can Dispel Any Evil

In this day and age, it is not possible for anyone to cultivate the Dharma free from adversity. Even noble beings who are close to attaining the first bodhisattva level still encounter all kinds of hardships and hindrances.

Yet so long as we do not lose confidence when we encounter misfortune, and if we steadfastly pray to our teacher and the Three Jewels and do not allow external circumstances to bind us, then we will definitely receive immense blessings and protection, and from there we will quickly attain liberation. In fact, once practitioners fully possess mindfulness within, nothing can harm them. The demon king Mara acknowledged this himself in front of the Buddha.

Ultimately speaking, the creators of obstacles do not have the ability to ruin a disciple of the Three Jewels. Therefore, as long as we have firm belief, even chanting the *Aspiration of Bodhisattva Samantabhadra* just once can dispel the harm of any evil. This is the precious teaching expounded by Shakyamuni Buddha.

To Counteract Harmful Speech,
Chant OM VAJRASATTVA HUM

A lot of people like to give others nicknames, calling them Big Nose, Small Eyes, Shorty, Fatty, and other names that are even more offensive. Actually, if you often call others Fatty, then in the next five hundred lives you might take birth as a fat person yourself, having carelessly committed unwholesome actions that you will later regret.

My root teacher Thupga Rinpoche often taught on the effect of name-calling and would cite a story in Patrul Rinpoche's *Words of My Perfect Teacher:* There was once a person who abused others by using the names of eighteen types of animal heads. Later he was reborn as a monster with the heads of eighteen animals.

As a matter of fact, the karma of speech is the easiest to produce, and thus the wise never speak carelessly. They often rely on the teachings of the noble ones to observe the timing, setting, and tone of their speech, and then they say only what is necessary.

In our daily lives we also need to be scrupulously cautious, control our tongues, and not willfully hurl harsh words at others. If because of the manifestation of your karma you lose control and swear at someone, you should immediately chant OM VAJRASATTVA HUM at least one thousand times, or even one hundred thousand times. Through the inconceivable blessing of this mantra you can purify any terrifying karmic obscuration.

Bodhichitta Can Dispel Any Negative Energy

Arousing bodhichitta and assimilating bodhichitta is an immensely profound spiritual path.

From a very young age, I took on studying and practicing the Buddhadharma as the focus of my life. I had the great fortune to follow, study under, and practice with over 130 extraordinary teachers. I also had the opportunity to teach the Buddhadharma to tens of thousands of people.

In my personal experience, among all the methods of Buddhist practice, the instruction on bodhichitta is extremely profound. Even merely listening to the teachings of this practice can sow seeds of liberation, to say nothing of the benefits of actually practicing bodhichitta.

If you can allow bodhichitta to permeate your daily life and practice, you will attain inconceivable benefits. Not only will it bring health, longevity, and abundance, it can also dispel your own and even all of society's various negative energies.

Do Not Let Yourself Be a Slave to Desires

The happiness that can be obtained from any worldly enjoyment is very meager, yet the suffering that ensues knows no bounds. Regrettably, however, many people do not seem to realize desire's multitude of faults. They remain indifferent to the flaws and helplessly wallow in desire day and night. During their youth, many people expend enormous energy to pursue unnecessary worldly enjoyments, believing they have a long life ahead of them. But in fact, a person's life is rather short. The elderly know this well.

From the age of one to the teens is a time of lighthearted childhood play. These years are like a dream, and they pass in a daze. The period from the teens to the forties could be viewed as life's golden age, but it too slips away in the blink of an eye. During this stage, people often face various family- and work-related obstacles and cannot afford the time to practice the virtuous Dharma. Once people reach their fifties and sixties, the body is not as it was. Although you wish to cultivate virtue and give up wrongdoing, by this time the spirit is willing but the flesh is weak. It is also too late to lament.

Hence, you must hold on to the time in front of you and not recklessly squander your precious life. In particular, when seductive desire has hooked your mind, you should employ various methods to recognize its true nature. Do not let yourself be a slave at its mercy anymore!

6

Triumph over Suffering

IF WE FALL ILL or endure inexplicable harm, we must not be filled with anger or hate. Recognize that this presents a good opportunity to practice tonglen, the meditation of exchanging self and other; it is a special empowering condition!

How to Cut Off the Suffering of Clinging to Another

When you feel fierce love toward another and the mind becomes extremely uneasy, what are the methods to calm the afflictions that arise from this?

Let us study one of Mipham Rinpoche's teachings and see how an old tantric yogi who was burning with desire absorbed the desire into a splendid practice by practicing the Great Perfection.

A long time ago, in a place called Lotus Land, there bloomed many fascinating and beautiful flowers. Here lived an old tantric yogi whose desire blazed like an inferno. Because of this, he was named Desire Inflamed.

One day, this old yogi met a beautiful maiden. There and then, it was as if his spirit had been whisked away. He rushed to her side, humbly prostrated at her feet, and begged her to live with him.

The maiden saw that this yogi was old and ugly. Not only was she unwilling to consort with him, she kicked him in the head and scolded him harshly: "Get lost!" Then she went to a youth called Young And Happy who was standing nearby and embraced him.

The old tantric yogi's wish was not fulfilled; instead, he was shamed and abused. Seeing the maiden and the youth acting like lovebirds made his desire even stronger. Eventually he lost his appetite and could not sleep at night. All day long he sighed.

Those around the old tantric yogi thought he was ill, so they sought out many famous doctors. Some doctors believed that his illness was caused by the wind element; others thought it was caused by the fire element or demons. Each gave him the relevant treatment. Yet not only were these methods ineffective, but they worsened his illness day by day.

Every day the old tantric yogi called out the maiden's name. His body deteriorated further, and in the end he went mad. During that time, kindhearted people invited many Dharma teachers to empower him and bless him, but all to no avail.

One day, the bodhisattva Manjushri appeared as the sixteen-year-old Moon Youth. A pleasing fragrance emanated from his mouth, and he came before the tantric yogi and said, "Dear old man, what is really the matter with you?"

As soon as he saw Moon Youth, the old yogi felt a sense of joy, and he regained his senses somewhat. He took the youth's hand and said, "As soon as I saw this beautiful maiden, an uncontrollable desire arose in me. Whenever I see her with another, looking upon him with love, I always secretly think how wonderful it would be if that were I! As these thoughts churned in my mind over and over, I ended up like this."

Moon Youth said, "Dear old man, you really should ponder this well! For you to feel love toward her is just like a moth being drawn to a flame. You should know that a maiden's youth is as ephemeral as a water lily. When the day comes when this beauty is aged and sallow, her face full of wrinkles, will you still be willing to love her as you do now? Neither do you realize that you are now silver-haired yourself, nor that her lovely body is inherently impermanent; you are truly under the influence of Mara. Please do not continue to cling to her. Cut off this craving!"

When he heard this, tears rolled down the old man's cheeks. "Alas, Moon Youth, you are certainly right, but it cannot change my heart. If you have any sympathy for me, please bring her to me. Even if I possessed all the world's riches, nothing else could satisfy me apart from this one wish. In this world, she alone can make me happy."

Moon Youth continued to reason with the old man. "You have sunken inextricably deep into something that is utterly meaningless. What is the point? Before you saw her, your mind was very pure. Yet since you laid eyes on her, you have behaved out of character. Your mind has been shot by the demon king's arrow of greed; you are really to be pitied. If everyone were like you and adored beautiful but unapproachable maidens, even refusing food out of disappointment, think how foolish that would be!

"When it comes to wishes that can never be realized and things that are completely unattainable, you should not insist on having them. Otherwise, they will inflict fierce suffering on your body and mind. Not only will you experience onslaughts of afflictions in this life, but you will also completely destroy your future lives.

"Before, you were a majestic tantric yogi. You could tame evil spirits, and people respected you. Yet the moment your own demon mind has appeared, you have no antidote for it. This is just ridiculous!

"Time and again, you cling to her flowerlike, moonlike beauty, believing her to be an unrivaled celestial creature. This is merely your discriminative mind."

Downcast, the old man mumbled, "You are perfectly right, but I still cannot forget her. It is as if there were a spike wedged in the depth of my heart. I simply cannot let go of my love for her."

Moon Youth said to him, "Dear old man, please listen to these words, which spring from my heart. You said that your mind is in love with her. Now then, let me tell you a story. It explains the best way to dispel suffering—using the mind to cut off your own craving.

"In the land of Alaya, a youth by the name of Discriminative Mind was crying. A passerby asked him, 'Why are you crying?'

"The youth said, 'I have seen a beautiful maiden, and I want her.'

"So this kind passerby consoled him. 'Please don't cry. The truth is that it is not this maiden who has tempted you, but your mind that has been distracted by external circumstances and has constricted you.

"'The mind is originally like empty space, without any suffering. But you insist on clinging to external objects, which is like tying a knot in empty space and deliberately producing all sorts of afflictions.

"'The pain of not having what we want originates from our mind. Clinging to a maiden is also like this. My son, if you can allow your mind to abide in peace and calm, then no one will have the power to harm or tempt you. On the contrary, if your mind is clinging desperately to external objects and unwilling to let go, this is like being trapped in a prison, and you will constantly endure all kinds of suffering.

"'Thus, please observe your mind carefully, and you will discover that it is inherently like empty space, without any thoughts of craving. In this manner, craving will be like darkness under the sun—it will naturally disperse into the expanse of reality.'

"You must know this technique of letting the mind naturally and calmly abide, and use it to cut your craving. In short, when craving is aroused, if you can instantly see its nature, it will disappear in that moment."

After hearing this, the old tantric yogi suddenly felt infinite peace and happiness, and his craving was completely uprooted. Brimming with gratitude, he said, "Moon Youth, you are truly a guide toward happiness. What a shame that I met you so late! In the past I have heard 'All phenomena are but the creations of the mind,' yet I only had a literal understanding and never truly practiced it. As a result, I have wasted most of my life in meaningless desires.

"My practice previously could not tame my mind; instead it allowed afflictions to grow greater and cravings to burn stronger. There are many tantric yogis like me. I hope you will use skillful means to truly impart these sublime teachings to those who mistakenly believe themselves to be tantric practitioners.

"I am deeply indebted to you. Now I know that 'relying on desire to seek liberation' is a fanciful delusion. Even though I am already old, desire still harmed me greatly. Meeting you today has added a rainbow to my merit. You are truly my immensely kind teacher!" Tears streamed down the old man's face, and he respectfully prostrated to Moon Youth.

Moon Youth continued to teach him. "I will give you another teaching. In the future, when you see a beautiful maiden and desire is aroused, you need to realize that this is in fact the glue that binds you to samsara. If you wish to transform craving into practice, you must first visualize the manifestation of all phenomena as your own mind. Know that the maiden is the manifestation of your mind, and then visualize the mind as emptiness. At this point, would a rainbow in empty space confine empty space? Certainly not. After this, observe that which can crave and that which is craved. You will discover that external objects and your mind are not different. Craving and external objects cannot fetter you at all.

"Once you realize this principle, it makes no difference if you look at a beauty or not. It is like stepping into fire in a dream and being completely unscathed. At this point you can transform everything you see into practice. You will not be like the ordinary people of the world who as soon as they see a beautiful maiden crave her and are bound to experience limitless suffering.

"If you can transform this craving into practice, you can meet with beautiful maidens or even be in further contact with them. Of course, you must first have the corresponding levels of realization. To a small lantern, a gale is an adversity, but to a forest fire it is actually a positive supporting condition. When the wind becomes stronger, the fire in the forest becomes fiercer. Hence, we should savor the felicitous details of the pith instructions according to the actual state of our wisdom body." (Among India's eighty-four *mahasiddhas* of the past, some acted according to the practice of neither adopting nor abandoning; they manifested as hunters, butchers, and prostitutes, but none of these guises could taint them in the slightest. However, these extraordinary actions of the noble ones cannot be carelessly mimicked by ordinary beings. Therefore, it is best for beginners to observe the pure precepts and not get lost in fancies and conjectures.)

Finally, Moon Youth earnestly enjoined the old tantric yogi, "After hearing my words, many who purport to be Tantrayana practitioners may fear falling into hell in the future. I hope that through this profound skillful teaching, they will attain liberation in the shortest time possible!"

Is Life Really a Dream?

People often say, "Life is like a dream." Is this truly the case? Everything that occurs around us clearly seems so real. The happiness and suffering that things bring us are also so evident. Why do we insist on saying that life is a dream?

To an ordinary person, being awake and dreaming are completely different: being awake is real; dreaming is not real. No one would cling to a dream as something that truly existed, yet everyone treats the things of their waking hours as real, and from this are born thousands of attachments and millions of sufferings. If being awake also had no true substance, just like a dream, then everything we cling to now would lose its meaning. But is this really the case?

Now, using Mipham Rinpoche's method, let us have a mock debate between waking and dreaming to look into the truth of these two.

Argument

The sly Awake spoke first. "Your dreams are not real!"

Honest Dreaming said, "Not only I—in reality you also are unreal!"

Round One

AWAKE: I definitely am not unreal. For example, when I eat meat, I can satisfy my hunger, and my body hurts when it is burned. These feelings truly exist.

DREAMING: Your argument does not stand. When I eat meat in a dream, I too feel full, and I also feel pain when burned. The sensations are exactly the same as yours.

Round Two

AWAKE: None of the things that appeared in your dream last night existed when you woke in the morning. Hence, you are not real.

DREAMING: Similarly, everything you feel today will not exist when tomorrow comes. Therefore, you also are not real.

Round Three

AWAKE: Granted, these will not be there tomorrow, but everything today has been experienced personally by me, so these things must be real.

DREAMING: If personal experience is the marker of reality, then the things I encounter in dreams are also personal experiences. How is that any different from you?

Round Four

AWAKE: Things that appear when I am awake are long-lasting and stable. For example, the furnishings in my house remain unchanged every day, so they must be real. Whereas your dreams disappear quickly, so they are a kind of illusion.

DREAMING: Not all scenes in dreams are brief; there are also long ones. For example, Tulku Shekun during one night of radiant dreaming enjoyed twenty-one years of life in a pure buddha field. I also have very long dreams, so you cannot use duration to distinguish real from unreal.

Round Five

AWAKE: In dreams one can freely pass through rocks and fly in the sky. In real life, do people have these abilities? Do you not admit that you are not real?

DREAMING: What's the big deal? So long as the necessary causes and conditions are present, even when you are awake you can also achieve all these things. For example, Master Padmasambhava showed several kings that he could remain unscathed by fire and not sink in water. When Venerable Milarepa was demonstrating his miraculous powers, he also freely passed through rocks and flew in the sky. When Khatok Dampa Deshek was a child, there were one hundred thousand *bhikshus* at Khatok Monastery. Each noon they went out for alms, and in the afternoon flew back to their own thatched rooms.

Hence, so long as the necessary causes and conditions—such as mantras, sacred objects, or meditative concentration—are present, it is also possible to manifest these miracles while awake. Conversely, if the causes and conditions are not sufficient, then even in dreams one cannot pass through mountains, walk on water, or fly with ease.

Round Six

AWAKE: Ah, but in dreams, these miracles can appear in the absence of causes and conditions. All you have to do is lie down on your bed and you start to dream. What causes and conditions are required? Do you not dream at will?

DREAMING: If causes and conditions are not needed, then why do you not dream of these things every night? The reason a particular phenomenon has not appeared is precisely that there are not sufficient causes and conditions. If all these things in dreams do not require causes and conditions, then it follows that they should appear constantly!

Round Seven

AWAKE: In dreams, friends who have died can be reunited; a son one never had can be born. These are not possible at all when one is awake. Thus you are definitely not real. This cannot be doubted.

DREAMING: Why is it not real just because it is different from your experience? You should treat things in dreams and in waking life equally. You cannot use your waking experience as the benchmark and jump to the conclusion that I am not real.

To you, so-and-so may have already died, but in my eyes, he is still alive and well, and we are able to meet. Bearing a son in a dream is impossible for you, but to me it can indeed happen. You cannot deem it unreal just because it is not in the realm of your awareness.

Round Eight

AWAKE: The delicacies enjoyed in a dream cannot prevent hunger when one wakes in the morning. Therefore, your dream is definitely not real.

DREAMING: By the same token, the grand and splendid palace you live in when awake cannot dispel the attack of a furious storm in a dream. Therefore, you also are not necessarily real.

Round Nine

AWAKE: Your dreams at night are in fact apparitions of delusion.

DREAMING: If everything in dreams is delusion, then what you encounter when awake is just the same! The same illustration applies.

Round Ten

AWAKE: After you dream at night, as long as you review it when you wake, you can realize that the dream was not real. But when you are dreaming, it is not at all possible to know that the things that appear when you are awake are not real.

DREAMING: So what? Are you saying that what I see in dreams is incorrect just because I am aware of different things than when you are awake? You maintain that I am not real because dreams do not exist when the dreamer wakes, but what you encounter when awake also does not exist in dreams. Why insist that you are real?

In short, if one is real, both are real. If one is not real, both are not real. The two of us have not the slightest distinction.

This play-like teaching has only briefly offered us a way of thinking. Of course, for the wise, this teaching alone is enough to realize the true nature of all phenomena.

Analyzing from different angles shows that there is indeed no difference between being awake and dreaming. That is to say, if seen in terms of absolute reality, neither of these two truly exists; otherwise, each has its own manifestation. If one is real, then both are real; if one is not real, then both are not real.

Once you realize this, whenever and wherever you are in your daily life, you ought to look deeply and reflect that all phenomena are like dreams, and not be too attached to anything. When you desire or hate another, immediately recognize that this is the same as hating an enemy or desiring a beloved in a dream. When you succeed or fail, also know that this is just like the failures and successes in dreams.

If you slowly give up attachments in this way, not only will you be free from all kinds of suffering, but you will also eventually see the true nature of all phenomena and attain the fruition of the Tathagata throughout the three times!*

* Tathagata (Skt.) is a title for the Buddha, literally "the one who has thus gone" or "the one who has thus come." The three times are the past, present, and future.

7

The Power of Right View

WHEN WORLDLY people practice Buddhism, if there is excessive comfort in all areas of their life, renunciation will not be easy. But if conditions are too harsh and they lack sufficient food or clothing, the body will experience unease. When the body is not at ease, the practice will not be fruitful. Thus, the Mahayana sutras and *shastras* say to avoid falling into the two extremes. One should practice the middle way.

Confidence and Right View Are the
Most Dependable Things in Life

Every individual must earnestly ponder the path ahead. For the present and the future to be perfect and happy, we must make haste and do things that will benefit us.

Of course, as I see it, what is of the most help to living beings' present and future lives is none other than the sublime Buddhadharma. There are two key points that are crucial in Buddhadharma. The first is pure view, especially the right view of belief in cause and effect. Without it, one will not attain the peace and happiness of the higher realms. The second is untainted confidence—that is, unfailing confidence in the Three Jewels. This is the foundation of all perfect attainment in this life and in future lives.

How important then are confidence in the Three Jewels and the right view of the truth of cause and effect? The Buddha told us that when we possess these two, we are assured of never falling to the lower realms. We can also attain all the virtue and merit we seek through these two.

Thus, confidence and right view are our ultimate friends. Things like wealth, position, and fame cannot be depended upon forever. None of these can be brought along with us in the bardo.

Our lives are like the stars at dawn, disappearing in the blink of an eye. As I am an old man, it is easier for me to have this insight. But those of you who are young should not think that the future is still long. Do not have this kind of blind self-confidence. Everyone needs to contemplate what plans he or she has for the future.

Even the Smallest Good Deed Can Bring Boundless Peace and Happiness

At the hands of death, the king and the beggar are equal. After death, every being will drift along in cyclic existence with the wholesome and unwholesome karma they have created. Therefore, it is extremely unwise to produce much unwholesome karma for the sake of gaining benefit in this life.

Everyone—no matter who it is—wishes to have happiness and not to have suffering. Thus, to gain long-lasting peace and happiness in the future, during this brief life of ours we should practice the authentic Dharma while the choice is still in our hands. Mipham Rinpoche said that this life is the seed and the next life is the fruit; since this is the way things are, why not do more virtuous deeds? If farmers tilling the land wish to harvest in fall, they must plow and sow well in spring.

I have repeatedly said that even the smallest good deed can yield immeasurable peace and happiness in the future. For instance, chanting the *Aspiration of Bodhisattva Samantabhadra* once every day takes only a little time, but through this virtue, you can definitely eradicate the root causes of the lower realms and attain infinite, wondrous peace and happiness in the future. And it is said in the sutras that if one hears just the sound of the conch before a Dharma teaching—let alone the actual Buddhadharma—one will not fall into the lower realms. Therefore, let us not think that small virtuous acts are insignificant. If you only crave the momentary pleasures of this life and never prepare for the future, you are sure to be filled with regret in old age.

Our mind residing in our body is like a small bird resting in a big tree: their time together is very short. Especially as we age, our hair is whitened, strand by strand, by the hardships of life, and we can no longer walk upright as we did in the past. This means the small bird is about to leave the big tree.

Thus, when the rare causes and conditions appear for the small bird of consciousness and this big tree of the body to come together, we must make haste and practice diligently!

When the Right Causes and Conditions Gather, the Fruit Must Ripen

The most basic criterion for being a Buddhist is to have a degree of understanding of and belief in cause and effect. If you have no confidence in cause and effect, then even if you cultivate the most profound Dharma, it will not have much of a result.

Everyone should first understand that retribution is caused by living beings' karma. Karma may be wholesome or unwholesome. With both types of karma, there is that which must ripen, that which may not ripen, that which must ripen in this life, and that which will ripen in a future life. Within this last type of karma there is also that which will ripen in the next life and that which will ripen in many lifetimes. Thus, living beings' experiences of karma differ in terms of time span and retribution.

Sometimes people believe, "If I do a good deed today, it will surely ripen immediately as a wholesome result; if I commit a harmful deed today, I will experience the negative result very soon." This belief comes from not understanding cause and effect. If there is true understanding, one should know that "when the right causes and conditions come together, their fruit must ripen."

There are also those who say, "Throughout my life I have chanted the name of Amitabha, meditated, and done many good deeds like making generous donations. Yet my mind is still overwhelmed with afflictions, my family life discordant, and my business unsuccessful. Where have the Three Jewels' blessings gone? Cause and effect must be false!"

This is a significantly wrong view. Even Shakyamuni Buddha never said that karma is sown and reaped in quick succession. Rather, he taught that it is "indestructible in one hundred aeons"—that is, even after one hundred aeons have passed, the karma will not disappear or be destroyed.

Someone might ask, "When Buddha was in the world, many people became enlightened as soon as they started to practice; also, wholesome and unwholesome karma were sown and reaped in one lifetime. Yet today, living beings' practices are not like that, and karmic retribution also cannot occur quickly. Why is this so?"

The reason is very simple. The era when the Buddha lived was the Dharma age of fruition; living beings at that time had the sharpest faculties, so as soon as they practiced, they attained enlightenment. In particular, attaining the Hinayana [foundational] levels of enlightenment happened very quickly. This, however, is the Dharma age of degeneration; living beings' faculties are clearly inferior to those of the past, and karmic ripening is also not as fast.

But even though this is so, the nature of karma does not change. It is still true that even after hundreds and thousands of aeons, the karma we have created will not be destroyed. As long as we earnestly practice now, sooner or later, we will obtain the corresponding fruits of attainment.

"If You Seek Worldly Trifles, There Will Never Be an End to Them"

In samsara, living beings chase after impermanent worldly concerns rather than seek liberation. As a result, they forever wallow in the ocean of suffering, bobbing up and down like bubbles on the surface of water.

In truth, worldly concerns are as momentary and impermanent as lightning; chasing after them will never have an end. It is just as Venerable Longchenpa said, "If you seek worldly trifles, there will never be an end to them. The moment you let go is the moment they end."

Since beginningless time, we have wasted incalculable energy on mundane concerns. But ultimately it has been futile. Thus, now is the time to give the mind a good rest.

Some people are very attached to everything in the world; even though they are very wealthy, they are not the slightest bit willing to lend a hand to those who need help. The truth is, people of despicable character can also obtain worldly fortunes that are tainted by clinging. Therefore, when we possess a little property, we must not be proud.

My teacher Thupga Rinpoche taught that the god of wealth once put on his best clothes and imperiously went to visit a god by the name of Konka. He discovered, however, that the god Konka's wealth far exceeded his. In that moment, his pride completely vanished.

If even the fortune of the god of wealth is nothing remarkable, what is there in our riches to be proud of? Hence, we should closely examine the impermanence of all phenomena, regard everything as being like dreams and illusions, and observe all worldly phenomena as if watching images on a screen. As time passes, our fierce attachments to people, events, and things will gradually fade to nothing, and all virtues and merits will naturally be attained.

Do Not Climb the Social Ladder Excessively

In order for life to progress well, you must not be overly concerned with climbing the social ladder in your daily life. If the body is engaged in myriad worldly activities, the mouth is emitting much idle speech, and the mind is continuously generating an endless stream of discriminating thoughts, you will bring immense difficulties upon yourself.

Hence, from this moment, you should discard meaningless things and practice the Buddhadharma, which has limitless merit and can tame your mind. If you rely on the instructions of a spiritual mentor and truly practice with diligence, even if it is only for a month, you will gain evident benefits.

Some people formerly had numerous opportunities to practice, but they found frequent excuses to postpone it, and thereby they exhausted all their excellent chances. There are others who have practiced for many years, yet on the inside, they have idled away their time in thrall to the afflictions. The thief of the afflictions has already robbed them of all their virtues. Their practice never showed any signs of progress. This is not because the Three Jewels have not blessed them but because their own unwholesome karma is too heavy or their diligence insufficient.

Therefore, it is best not to follow after distractions, afflictions, or unwholesome thoughts. Rather, we should completely abandon them, or we will never find tranquillity.

Of course, if you wish to be enlightened rapidly, that is also not very likely. But the truth of dependent origination does not deceive. I believe that as long as you remain diligent and rely on the strength of unfailing dependent origination, you will be assured of receiving the corresponding merit. Everything in your present and future lives will be auspicious, and you will not meet with any adversity.

Stay Clear of the Despicable

In this day and age, there are fewer and fewer people who are worthy of trust. Thus, when we are carrying out important endeavors, we should not publicize it casually but do things in a discreet way so that we are less likely to encounter obstacles. We must be able to be fierce in our actions and possess magnetizing abilities. Be compassionate to our own, be courageous when facing an enemy, and be able to discriminate between the good and bad in others' actions.

Looking at history, we see that the tragic, violent suffering of many was sometimes caused by the evil actions of just one or two people. Hence, these kinds of villains, especially those who have committed irredeemably evil deeds, must immediately be cast out. Otherwise they will destroy their community and their nation.

Within Buddhism, if living beings of extremely despicable character cannot be tamed using gentle means, then with compassion and loving-kindness, buddhas and bodhisattvas must employ fierce actions to subdue them. This also conforms to worldly rules. In the teachings of many rulers, it is said that for villains who are unwilling to repent and change, apart from slashing and killing the body, any other punishments such as constraint and whipping are permitted. If a king sentences a person to death, that king's Dharma teacher ought to speak out and persuade him against it. But if a king uses other means to punish, then the Dharma teacher does not need to stop him.

As you can see, for a nation's safety and for all living beings' peace and happiness, sometimes it is necessary to take drastic action against contemptible beings.

.

8

When You Ask for Directions,
Ask Those Who Have Gone Before

WHEN WE JUDGE someone or something, we must not observe and judge with the views of a worldly person. We really need to be prudent!

Do not praise evil people. If a person is not a great master, do not tout him or her as one. However, you should not ridicule authentic great masters at will, or presume to speculate about them and slander them with a worldly mind.

Our Teacher's Kindness Surpasses the Buddha's

Be they senior teachers or junior ones, renowned teachers or unknowns, so long as we have received the Buddhadharma from them, they are our gurus. For this, we ought to remain eternally grateful.

During the time of Shakyamuni Buddha, one venerable bodhisattva renounced samsara under the guidance of Bhikshu Mahanaman, who was one of Buddha's five earliest disciples. Later, when this bodhisattva saw Bhikshu Mahanaman together with Buddha, he first prostrated to Bhikshu Mahanaman, his direct teacher, and then to Shakyamuni Buddha. Upon seeing this, Buddha praised him profusely: "Your conduct is correct! You should always first pay homage to the teacher whose kindness you have received."

Bhikshu Mahanaman's wisdom and virtue certainly did not compare to those of Buddha. But Buddha said this to remind everyone never to forget the kindness of his or her guru.

Truly wise people know that even the most minimal states of realization they attain are not due solely to their own efforts but occur through the compassionate blessings of their teacher. They feel deeply grateful for their teacher's kindness and always show this with their words.

In contrast, people of lowly character consider only renowned and wealthy teachers to be their own teacher. When it comes to authentic, qualified Dharma teachers who are content and crave little, even if the students have received many teachings from them, they are unwilling to admit it. To be so secretive about one's own unknown guru yet brag about a famous one is really ridiculous behavior.

When these people receive sublime teachings, they never consider it to be through the kindness of their teacher. Instead, they believe that it is due to their own unparalleled wisdom and merit and that it has nothing whatsoever to do with their teacher. In the beginning, they are reverent and respectful to their teacher; as soon as they have received teachings, they discard their teacher. It is like some patients who turn a cold shoulder to their doctor as soon as they are healed.

This is not a true Dharma vessel. Such foolish people are full of pride; they do not know the sublime nature of teachers and have completely forfeited their conditions for enlightenment. No matter how great their ability to understand or how broad their knowledge, they will never gain any spiritual attainment.

Respect for One's Teacher Cannot Be Mere Lip Service

Respect for one's teacher is shown not by outer actions but by the heart. For instance, Mipham Rinpoche once had an attendant by the name of Lama Ösel. In the beginning, Lama Ösel was a fool with a fiery temper. Even in front of his teacher, he acted very rude, and his attitude was not gentle or reverent at all. Occasionally, Mipham Rinpoche gave personal permission for disciples to come see him. Yet Lama Ösel would stop them at the door and claim that Rinpoche was severely ill. No matter what, he refused to allow them in.

Mipham Rinpoche himself also seemed to be scared of this attendant. One time, Khenpo Yönga came to seek Rinpoche's advice, as Khenpo was composing teachings on the *Treasury of Precious Qualities*. Mipham Rinpoche was about to explain many profound teachings when Ösel came in. Rinpoche became very nervous and hurriedly said to Khenpo Yönga, "Quick, go home! Ösel is here, I do not dare to teach you now."

On the surface, Ösel seemed particularly disrespectful to his teacher. But in fact, he was deeply concerned for Rinpoche and worried that he toiled too hard as he carried on benefiting living beings while ill. Because of this devotion and faith, in the end, all of his teacher's wisdom was passed onto Ösel.

Before Mipham Rinpoche died, he said to Ösel, "If you meet with difficulties in the future, go find Pelmo Khyentse." Rinpoche also said to the others, "If he falls ill in the future, you must care for him!"

Thus, superficial flowery, clever words are not important. To see how disciples actually treat their teacher, the key is to see if they have true confidence, reverence, and fondness.

When Seeking Teachers, Do Not Judge Them by Their Appearance

When fools make friends, they often consider others' wealth, position, and appearance. It seems that nowadays, seeking teachers is also like this. If the teachers' parents are distinguished, and they themselves appear rather dignified, then many people would like to be their disciple.

In ancient times, tulkus were not necessarily elegant and dignified in appearance. Take the famous Master Butön, who founded the Zhalu lineage. At birth, his mouth and nose were both huge and incredibly ugly. His mother was very sad: "I have only this one child, but he is so repulsive. Who would wish to see him?" Unexpectedly, the baby opened his mouth and said, "Butönpa [literally, 'this child can be seen by anyone'], I do not care about these at all!" In the end, he grew up to be one of the most eminent monks of his age.

In the history of the Geluk tradition, there were also many eminent monks and masters who were far from handsome.

If you are looking for a wife, it is all right to choose a good-looking one. But when it comes to following a master, this is not really necessary. Judging by appearance is a fool's method of observation. As someone with wisdom, you ought to place greater value on the inside than the outside—only after you have carefully examined a teacher's compassion and wisdom should you decide whether or not to follow that teacher. This is the more reliable way.

Do Not Be Enamored with the New and Tired of the Old

In the old days, the Venerable Atisha followed many teachers in his life. Some of these teachers' virtues were greater than his, some equal to his, and some inferior to his. But no matter what, he was full of gratitude toward each teacher and very reverent. By contrast, Dromtönpa had only two teachers in his life: one was a lay Dharma teacher, and one was Venerable Atisha.

Later, Putowa asked his teacher Dromtönpa, "Is it better to be like you and follow few teachers or to be like Venerable Atisha and follow many?"

Dromtönpa told him, "If you have cultivated a pure mind, then the more teachers you follow, the better. But if your mind is not sufficiently pure and you are always looking for your teacher's flaws, then the fewer teachers you follow, the better."

These days, many people will rush to honor and make offerings to a teacher as soon as they meet him or her. Yet they soon begin to feel that this teacher has many flaws, so they reject and may even slander their teacher. There are also people who frequently test their teacher; they think of one thing but will say another. If you behave in this manner, it will not benefit you in the slightest no matter how many teachers you follow.

Hence, for most people, it is enough just to follow a few teachers in one's life. Do not always be fond of the new and quickly tire of the old, seeking out "fresh" teachers everywhere!

Only with Lineage Is There Power

In this world, myriad professions have their own teachers and lineages. Similarly, in Buddhism, the traditions of the Sutrayana and the Vajrayana both place great value on lineage. Lineage is not only the continuation of Dharma transmission but also an invisible force of blessing.

In particular, the essence of Shakyamuni Buddha's eighty-four thousand methods of practice is none other than the Great Perfection. The transmission of the Great Perfection has continued from the *dharmakaya* buddha Samantabhadra to masters such as Master Padmasambhava and Vimalamitra, all the way to my present root teacher. These generations of teachers, through the means of bestowing empowerments and transmitting teachings, have allowed the transmissions that are pure and untainted like gold to be passed down continuously.

As a teacher of a lineage, apart from having personally received empowerments and listened to teachings, one must also have a degree of direct realization of the profound instructions. If within a lineage system there was never a person who slandered his or her teacher or broke the vows, then this is a pure lineage.

We must receive teachings from a teacher who is from a pure lineage. Some people do not value lineage; they even rely on teachings without a lineage and then believe that they are enlightened. But if wise ones were ever to meet these so-called enlightened beings, they would surely keep their distance, albeit respectfully.

There are certain people who had very deep connections with the Great Perfection in the past. Consequently, in this life, as soon as they come across related teachings, wisdom naturally arises in them. Of course, this is rather rare. However, even if they have already attained enlightenment through this teaching, they still must appear to follow teachers. It is just like Master Padmasambhava, who had already directly seen the dharmakaya but in life still followed countless teachers.

Hence, regardless of how famous an eminent monk or master may be, he or she must still follow teachers and then receive the pure transmissions.

Some Things Should Be Kept Secret

As a Vajrayana practitioner, you must keep secret the meditation deity and mantra of your practice, otherwise you will not attain any spiritual accomplishments. Yet nowadays, quite a few people do not understand this principle. They often discuss with others that their meditation deity is the bodhisattva Avalokiteshvara or the bodhisattva Manjushri. This is extremely foolish behavior.

In fact, secrecy is necessary not only for practice; even some medical treatments require secrecy or they will not have a significant effect. For instance, in the Tibetan medical system there is a type of medicine that treats lung diseases. After it has been collected, it is soaked in milk for one month, and it can cure chronic illnesses like tuberculosis. But the name of this medicine must be kept secret. When teachers instruct their students, they say only that there is such a medicine, and then gradually they describe its color, its shape, and where it grows. When they go into the mountains to gather it, if they spot some, the teacher will immediately hint to the students, "Look, here is a splendid medicine—what do you think it is?" If the students are clever enough, they will recognize it right away.

In the past, Desi Sangye Gyatso was a well-known medical expert throughout Tibet. He recorded a superb collection of "secret medicines" in one medical text and used secret codes to represent the uses of some types of Tibetan medicine.

Once, when I had heart trouble, a Tibetan doctor in Serthar gave me a packet of medicine and told me that I must not take it while on the road or I might fall asleep. Later I asked a number of people what it was. One doctor at the time told me that there used to be a type of Tibetan medicine made from pseudo-ginseng, which seemed to be quite similar to what I had. As soon as I knew this, its effect seemed to disappear. Hence, sometimes patients should not ask too many questions about certain things. If you can follow the doctors' advice, it will certainly be of benefit to you.

In Tibetan medicine, when a patient asks for the name of a certain medicine that needs to be kept secret, the name cannot be casually uttered. If both the doctor and patient can keep a secret, then this medicine's effects will be rapid and strong.

If even an efficacious medicine needs to be kept secret, then this is certainly true of the rare and precious Vajrayana teachings. In particular, when it comes to the sublime pith instructions of the generation stage and perfection stage, you should practice them secretly—even if they are well known. If you can follow your teacher's instructions and maintain strict secrecy about what needs to be kept secret, then you will definitely attain spiritual accomplishments!

Do Not Slander Bodhisattvas

There are many noble ones in this world who are transforming and liberating beings through their compassion and the strength of their aspiration. To others, it appears that they also experience suffering and happiness, fall ill, age, and have afflictions. But in reality, within their realm of awareness, these impure phenomena do not exist at all. It is pointed out in the *Supreme Continuum*, "The noble ones are free from all suffering, birth, old age, illness, and death." The *Adornment of Mahayana Sutras* also says, "When a bodhisattva has penetrated the emptiness of beings and things, to liberate sentient beings is like strolling in a garden: there is not any suffering."

There are even times when in order to benefit particular kinds of beings, the noble ones would present appearances that were worse than ordinary beings. We cannot casually slander these actions of theirs.

There was once a greatly accomplished master by the name of Jigme Phuntsok Jungne. Every summer, he often went on alms rounds in the Sershul area and was intimate with a girl there called Dijaja. Once when he was conferring a great empowerment on thousands of devotees, he saw that this girl had also arrived. So he casually left the ceremonial vase in midair, and with no hesitation, he carried the girl to his Dharma throne.

Since he was remarkably famous in his former lives, everyone remained very respectful initially and did not dare to find any fault with him. Yet his various actions seemed to deviate so far from those of a monk that later, many people's view of him dimmed.

During the period before he died, his actions became even crazier, to the point where even the monastery threw him out. When he was close to death and could not leave his bed because of severe illness, his disciples also did not carefully tend to him. He constantly shouted in great pain. His disciples were so ashamed that to avoid being ridiculed, they banged on instruments to cover up his awful cries.

After he died, people went to seek the advice of the celebrated Do Khyentse Yeshe Dorje. Do Khyentse Rinpoche asked everyone not to tell anyone else, took a gun, and shot it toward the ball of Jigme Phuntsok Jungne's foot, and a plume of smoke rose from the crown of his head. Afterward,

Do Khyentse Rinpoche said, "The great bodhisattva did not know yet that he had entered parinirvana. Only after my action was he aware. Now, he has abided it again." Later, Jigme Phuntsok Jungne was reborn as Tulku Tenpe Nyima. Once, he saw his dakini from his former life and recognized her instantly. He said, "She has aged, but her beauty has not diminished much." And also, "I can recall only my dakini from my former life, but not anything else. Why is this so?" He was just like that, often mocking himself.

During his lifetime, many of Jigme Phuntsok Jungne's actions were not in accord with the Dharma, which brought him a lot of criticism. But this does not mean that he really had faults. In truth, those faults were merely the games he played in front of people, just like an unpredictable and ever-changing dance.

At times, these great bodhisattvas seemed to be abandoning the precepts; at times, they seemed to feign madness and act like idiots. But there is no doubt that their actions had profound meanings that were difficult for ordinary people to fathom. Therefore, we must not recklessly hold wrong views!

Are All Shastras Worthy of Respect?

The Buddhist teachings that came from Shakyamuni Buddha are called sutras; the teachings that were composed after the Buddha's parinirvana by eminent monks and masters throughout history are referred to as shastras. Of course, the sutras definitely have inconceivable merit. As for the shastras by eminent monks, masters, and noble ones, although the

Buddha himself did not speak them, if they conform to Buddha's profound and hidden meanings, then we should also respect them as if Buddha spoke them.

Perhaps some will ask, "Then are all shastras worthy of respect?" The answer is *not necessarily*! If people have not thoroughly understood the Buddhist sutras and shastras but travel around spreading the Buddhadharma and writing commentaries, this does not necessarily benefit them or others.

According to Buddhist teaching, a shastra creator must meet one of three conditions: A superior creator must be a bodhisattva on the first level or above; an average one must have directly seen his or her meditation deity; and a basic one must be thoroughly versed in the five traditional sciences. Unless these conditions are met, then even if one has written voluminous and all-encompassing compositions, these shastras still cannot lead beings away from suffering and toward happiness.

Then, do followers debate over the shastras created by bodhisattvas on the first level or above? There is surely no shortage of disputes. For instance, regarding the shastras composed by Master Tsongkhapa, Venerable Milarepa, as well as many highly accomplished masters in the Jonang and Sakya traditions, there remains much disagreement today. But I believe that for us ordinary people, given our limited wisdom, to refute the teachings of noble bodhisattvas would be like the crow that tries to disguise itself as a great condor—we couldn't possibly succeed.

Anyone who wishes to create a shastra must not harbor the selfish intention of seeking fame and fortune. This is also true for teaching, debating, studying, and practicing the Dharma. Otherwise, without pure altruism, even though one may go through the motions of doing good deeds, everything done with that impure mind will be utterly meaningless. Only if one has eliminated all self-interest before beginning to spread the Dharma or study the Buddhist teachings would the merit dispel all adversities like the nectar of *devas*.

No Rainbow Is Worth Chasing After, No Matter How Beautiful

There are always people in the world who do not have any practical experience themselves but can spout an endless flow of eloquent words, amazing and beguiling those who do not know the truth.

It is like someone who has never been to Bodh Gaya in India but, using facts gleaned from television or photographs, starts to give a detailed description of Bodh Gaya to others. What such a person says cannot possibly convey the essence of the place, nor is it trustworthy. But if a person has been to Bodh Gaya, then even if she were not an eloquent speaker, I would trust that every sentence she says is quite accurate.

Spreading the Buddhadharma is similar to this. If teachers have even a little experience and realization through practice, they will not lead living beings down a wrong path. Otherwise, like a mimicking parrot, they merely echo what the books say, and their listeners do not receive any true benefit. Patrul Rinpoche also said, "If one has not the slightest personal understanding or realization, then reading the sutras and teaching the Dharma to others has little point."

According to legend, the beautiful rainbows in the sky are the bows of the gods. But when we seek them, we gain nothing. Similarly, the flowery and clever words of an ordinary being may fit well with the mind-set of other ordinary beings, sounding sonorous and alluring; yet, as they contain not an iota of true practice or realization, they will not bring much nourishment.

Only the Buddhadharma taught by practitioners who have truly realized the nature of the mind can unerringly guide living beings toward liberation!

9

Who Is the True Field of Merit?

WE SHOULD ESTABLISH an attitude of respect and admiration for our teachers. We need to understand what teachers represent. Why do they exert themselves to practice the Buddhadharma?

Stop Destroying Buddhism in the Name of Buddhism

When you make even the most modest offering to a monk or nun, you should choose one who is an authentic spiritual master. Do not blindly trust scheming crooks.

Lala Chudzi Rinpoche once pointed out, "People with scant virtue and merit, even if they wish to offer their possessions, cannot encounter a true field of merit."* This is truly a golden saying.

Nowadays, many people tend not to discriminate between true and false, so it is hard for them to meet a great, authentic

---

* Field of merit (Skt. *punyakshetra,* Tib. *tshogs zhing*): The focus or object of prayers, prostrations, and other offerings.

spiritual mentor. When they meet wise monks and nuns who uphold pure precepts and live simply, not only do they feel no respect, but they scoff and dismiss them. Instead they admire crafty rogues who talk at random and brag about their supposed supernatural powers.

Venerable Milarepa told his disciple Rechungpa, "In this age, wise ones are not respected, but fools are hailed. The Buddhadharma of true meaning is not valued, but the teachings of expedient meaning are lauded. Thus, you must endeavor to follow authentic spiritual mentors and seek instructions with real meaning." This advice applies to us today as well.

As we look at current trends, we see that some people have the title of Khenpo or Tulku, but in reality they do not cherish the Buddhadharma. They only know to pursue various worldly pleasures. Those who have compassion for living beings are as rare as stars at dawn. The ones who purport to be eminent monks and virtuous masters frequently cheat living beings with various excuses, and boldly amass wealth. Yet many people actually start to jostle to make offerings to these so-called masters without examining them closely. These people even boast of their "merit" everywhere they go.

This phenomenon is truly the sorrow of Buddhism, the sorrow of the monastic sangha, and the sorrow of the faithful! It is exactly these repellent actions that have propelled the Buddhadharma into the Dharma age of degeneration, and destroyed Buddhism's noble place in people's hearts.

In This Degenerate Age, a Demon Resides in Every Mind

In the past, most people were of noble character and rarely cheated others. As soon as they did something wrong, they immediately felt ashamed and instantly repented. Most of them took great care to guard their reputations and were willing to sacrifice their precious lives to honor their vows. Yet nowadays, many people use all sorts of crooked means to achieve their personal goals. Sometimes for the most insignificant gain, they are willing to betray their family and flout the law.

The ancients usually harbored gratitude to those who had given them care and help, and always remembered them steadfastly. When the causes and conditions were ripe, noble aristocrats and simple country folk alike knew to "repay the kindness of a drop of water with a fountain." Today, however, not only are people unable to behave in this way, but they even return kindness with animosity.

The ancients were amenable to others' different opinions and accepted sincere advice. People today, however, cannot tolerate any harsh criticism, even if sincerely offered, but are only prepared to hear the sounds of praise. For many people, being flattered is like tasting ambrosia, and they float on clouds of pride. As a result, their awareness of themselves and their surroundings becomes further distanced from reality.

In the past, when people met, they were mild-mannered, humble, polite, and considerate in their language. Yet people now mostly mingle out of self-interest. Even if there is no animosity at the beginning, not long after they meet, in-explicable conflicts and displeasure arise, followed by fierce anger. The root cause of this trouble is that people's personal interests are at odds.

Furthermore, it is not only between individuals that these difficulties occur. In the past, there was harmony between tribes and between countries, but it is exactly the opposite now. Many countries and regions in the world have erupted into conflict, and the flames of war rage everywhere. So-called peacetime is not so peaceful after all. Echoing this, in society, most people are wary in their interactions, and they scheme against one another. The entire community is per-vaded by an atmosphere of open and covert strife.

All these signs of chaos in the world have come to fulfill Master Padmasambhava's prophecy: During the Dharma age of degeneration, a demon resides in the minds of all men and women, old and young. This is not caused by changes in the environment but by living beings' actions that tend toward the heinous.

Where There's Buddhadharma, There's a Way

When we judge something, we should maintain a clear mind at all times. We should first use the wisdom of the Buddha-dharma to observe and to discern, and then bring worldly methods to bear.

Yet often when people come up against things, they only listen unthinkingly to their selfish minds or the discriminative thoughts of others. Then they echo others' opinions and rarely have their own independent views, let alone implement the Buddhadharma.

The omniscient Mipham Rinpoche particularly emphasized that no matter what we do, it must be done with wisdom. If we ourselves lack this ability, then we should seek the guidance of those who have good sense. Only after carefully weighing the pros and cons should one then act.

As a practitioner, if you wish to accomplish anything, on the one hand you should seek the advice of your teacher and also ask for the blessings of the Three Jewels. On the other hand, you need to analyze the situation with care and repeatedly reflect upon it. Only then can the final decision be considered a wise one that will not harm you or others. If, on the contrary, you are a law unto yourself in whatever you do, make yourself the center of everything, and willfully act without consideration, then your endeavors are unlikely to succeed and might even bring countless troubles, leading you to the abyss of suffering in the end.

Be Vigilant against Deceitful Monks and Nuns

Of the various signs of the Dharma age of degeneration, most appear with respect to monks and nuns. There are some monks and nuns who are monastics in appearance only. They believe that if they gain a little social status, they can become eminent masters. These people never study, reflect, or practice the Dharma, nor do they have even a modicum of virtue. Some of them even lack the most basic Buddhist knowledge. While their actions cause great amusement, we cannot help lamenting for the future of Buddhism.

The sutras record that as early as the time of Kashyapa Buddha,[*] there was a King Kriki who dreamed of an elephant. Its body was outside a window, but for a long while its tail refused to come out of the building. What is the meaning of this dream? It foreboded that during the final age of Shakyamuni Buddha's era, although many monastics had taken vows with their body, their minds were still reluctant to leave behind the eight worldly dharmas.

There is a story about one such monk. On his alms rounds, he asked a family if their life was peaceful. The master of the house answered, "Very much so!" Surprisingly, when the monk heard this, he was greatly disappointed. Why? It is because if this family had just lost a relative, this would have been an opportunity to chant sutras and perform transference for the dead. Then he could have received monetary offerings. Practitioners like this have hearts of such evil that their conduct will definitely lead them farther and farther from liberation.

Yet the more ignorant these people are, the more arrogant they tend to be. When they have the opportunity to meet an authentic master, not only do they feel no respect whatsoever, but they act arrogant and rude and treat the master with contempt. On the surface, they have shaved their heads to

---

[*] Kashyapa Buddha was the buddha who preceded Shakyamuni Buddha in this aeon.

become monks and nuns and abandoned their small worldly homes. In reality, however, they are building and defending an even bigger "fame and fortune" home!

Beware of Deluded Practitioners

In this day and age, there are very few authentic spiritual mentors with the characteristics of a dharmic person. Instead, proper conduct that accords with the Dharma has become a target for public censure.

Look around us. Many temples have turned into lay community centers and are no different from any noisy place in a city. If the conditions for study, reflection, and practice do not exist in a Buddhist practice center, how can it be called a sacred place for liberation? Some Dharma teachers in these lively temples do not try to spread the Dharma to benefit beings, nor do they observe pure precepts; instead, they greedily amass followers who make monetary offerings. In this way, how can one see hope for the spread of the authentic Dharma?

There is another group of people, who have never followed any teacher or cultivated any practices, but publicly peddle "Buddhadharma" to others. This is like stumbling around in the pitch-dark night with your eyes shut, yet also harboring a misleading intention of "guiding" others. Nowadays, there is a glut of these Dharma teachers who appear to be virtuous masters. They deceive themselves and others, talk carelessly without restraint, and have guided innumerable believers down wrong paths.

The main reason for this phenomenon is that people today do not value the Buddha's true teachings at all. Their understanding of the Buddhadharma is based only on their discriminating minds' judgments; they almost never rely on the teachings of the buddhas and bodhisattvas. This has allowed some ignorant and incompetent people to wedge themselves into the cracks and deceive beings everywhere.

The Most Solemnly Sworn Words Tend to Be Lies

Some people have immense greed for wealth. To satisfy their selfish greed, they can be clever and eloquent, and only beautiful lies flow from their mouths.

For instance, if they see an exquisite, luxurious bowl in someone's home, they will use all means possible to make it their own, persisting until they have attained their goal. They might first direct some artful talk at the owner, praising the bowl's exquisite craftsmanship, its long history, and so on. Then they would flatter the owner, saying how gracious and noble he is. After this, they might present all sorts of evidence to prove they have an intimate connection to the owner, almost like family. Finally, they would solemnly vow that if the owner were to make a gift of the bowl, in the future they would wholeheartedly support him, even leaping into a boiling cauldron or a blazing fire for this profound debt of gratitude.

The fact is, if the owner were to trust them and make a gift of the bowl, they would instantly banish from their mind every word just uttered—never mind repaying the debt of gratitude! In another scenario, if they were to find out that someone urgently needed some funds, they would do everything possible to meddle and obstruct the matter.

When people like this are in pursuit of certain possessions, they will flatter and praise others; when others acquire something new, however, their jealousy erupts immediately. Whatever they do, they are full of cunning and deceit. These behaviors are truly detestable!

Compassion and Wisdom, the Only Standard for Judging a Spiritual Mentor

Some monks and nuns will become self-righteous and arrogant beyond measure when they gain a little fame in society. They believe their conduct is entirely correct and they no longer need anyone's criticism or advice. These people tend to be shallow and ignorant, and they are unworthy of their titles. Yet quite a few blind followers have gathered around them.

As I see it, most people today do not really have the ability to discriminate between the wise and the foolish. Very few have the wisdom to recognize able people. Why is this so? It is because people no longer value the inner realization and merit of Buddhadharma. Instead, they only set store by a master's appearance and reputation.

With the passing of time, this has become the rule. Monastics who stray from the precepts and behave improperly are often seen as free and unrestrained enlightened ones. When their behavior clearly violates the precepts, some insist that these are unique skillful means. Cunning and devious characters are seen to possess extraordinary wisdom; fierce and cruel ones are even praised as being "full of heroic spirit"; those who maliciously slander others and sow discord are perversely lauded as eloquent and expressive.

In truth, the only way to evaluate spiritual mentors is to examine their inner wisdom and compassion. Do they have the compassion to sacrifice themselves for all beings under the sky, the wisdom that realizes the true nature of the expanse of reality?

Regrettably, the world always deviates from this standard; intentionally or not, it is swayed by ignorant and deluded views.

Do Not Be Intoxicated by Trivial States of Realization

Since beginningless time, the root causes that have led beings to continue to wallow in the boundless sea of suffering are the five poisonous afflictions. They are the enemies that harm our present and future lives. Therefore, what we most need to do now is to observe our mind continually, not let these afflictions control us, and not place value on superficial behavior.

Some people appear to reside in a quiet place and put on a show of teaching the Buddhadharma. In their minds, however, the five poisonous afflictions have not lessened at all. These people consider themselves quite extraordinary, but they do not realize that their actions have very little meaning.

These days, some people are so simple. When they see an impressive, glamorously dressed stranger, they become convinced that this person must possess extraordinary states of awareness; without any further examination, they blindly become followers. These same people have little respect for diligent practitioners who observe pure precepts and who possess remarkable wisdom. This is a lamentable thing. It is exactly as the omniscient Longchenpa said: When the wise and virtuous are not held in esteem, yet affected and ignorant ones are immensely honored, this is a mark of the Dharma age of degeneration!

When these shallow, foolish people are respected by others, their arrogance also increases. Like pouring gasoline on a fire, eventually it can only harm others without benefiting themselves.

In reality, no one is clearer about one's state of realization than oneself. So rather than readily believe others' praise, you should frequently look into your own mind. It is just as one virtuous master said: When we are praised by others, if what is said is within reason, then there is no need to rejoice. If it is not within reason, then the praise is false and insubstantial—and there is even less cause to be pleased with oneself.

Thus, we need to observe our mind constantly and not deceive ourselves or others. It would be a great shame if, having obtained this precious human form, we squandered most of our life chasing fame and fortune while having scarcely any true kindness within us!

There Are Many Types of Tulkus

Nowadays, sometimes ordinary people become great tulkus overnight. How can this be? Please ask these people, "Are you truly the reincarnation of an eminent monk or master?" If they are, then it is perfectly understandable that they are recognized as tulkus. If, however, they clearly know that they are not but continue to deceive living beings sanctimoniously, then they have definitely broken the precept against major lies. In ancient India, for example, until practitioners had attained the realization of an arhat, they were not permitted to sit on a yellow floral cushion.

These days, we frequently hear that this or that person is a tulku. The truth is, there are genuine ones and fake ones among these tulkus. People acknowledge fake tulkus either because they hope to exploit the connection for their family and friends or to gain social status. Even some monasteries recognize tulkus just to pursue fame, fortune, and the rest of the eight worldly dharmas.

These so-called tulkus have little practice experience, but after their title is bestowed, they become self-righteous and do not behave like practitioners at all. In contrast, some khenpos clearly are reincarnations of tulkus, but they never admit it. Adopting a low profile in this way is very good.

In fact, tulkus are divided into several types:

1. Before dying, sometimes eminent monks and masters give blessings to their future rebirth. Through proph-

ecies or dream omens, they bless someone who is not actually their reincarnation to be their nominal tulku. But this is not a tulku in the true sense.

2. Some people are not tulkus, but to benefit beings or for other hidden purposes, they are recognized as tulkus through certain methods.

3. There are also some tulkus who adopted it as the path during the bardo.

4. Some tulkus are under the influence of Mara. For instance, a demon who killed a teacher in a former life takes the form of the teacher, then directly changes into someone, or blesses someone and says, "This is the reincarnated tulku of our teacher."

In short, it is best that someone who is not a tulku does not masquerade as one. If you are truly virtuous, no one will belittle you. But if you believe that by just mimicking well you can really become a tulku, that is taking it too far!

I Am Not a Tulku

Many worldly people today like to pay respect to tulkus. While this activity has its merit, I hope that before you follow a tulku, you will carefully assess this tulku from several aspects. Do not readily believe whatever talk you have heard.

People say that I am the reincarnation of Tulku Lerab Lingpa. But I have never—not in the light of day or even in dreams—thought myself that I am this accomplished master. There are plenty of people who are as inferior as I am, some even more pathetic. In reality, what purpose is there for one to receive an undeserved title of Tulku? I hope some of you will reflect on this carefully.

In the past, many masters were honored as tulkus, but they did not then become pleased with themselves. They just quietly protected their virtue and merit. Other masters did not wish for the title of Tulku, but their teaching to benefit beings flourished unimpededly. There are people today, however, who believe themselves to be "tulkus" and smugly bask in others' praise. They go as far as drinking and smoking all day, craving women frequently, and satisfying their greed with the funds they obtain. To witness this abominable image of worldly defilement truly inspires pity.

Some immoral characters shamelessly boast of being tulkus in order to win respect and obtain offerings. They say to others, "Tulkus are the most noble! A tulku's status in Tibetan Buddhism is the highest!" Many people end up being taken in by these claims and believe that they can follow anyone who is a "tulku," even if this so-called tulku has not the slightest virtue. But when these people meet a teacher without a tulku title—no matter how sublime the teacher's virtue or how vast the teacher's knowledge, and even if all the Dharma characteristics of a spiritual guide are present—they cannot feel a drop of respect for this teacher.

This phenomenon is rather common in the Han regions and has now become a complex issue. Some fake tulkus have indeed inflicted deep and lasting harm on Tibetan Buddhism.

"If One's Mind Has Not Become a Demon, Then There Is Not a Single Outer Demon"

In the present era, there are many people with loose tongues who tell others, "I can see a spirit here, a demon there—we must practice a wrathful method to subdue them."

These people may be under the influence of Mara or have broken their precepts; as a result, they are in a confused state of mind and talk nonsense wherever they go. This brings great harm to Buddhism. We need to have a precise understanding of the effects of actions, and we must never foster these wrong views that contradict the Dharma. Otherwise, as this continues, we will be surrounded by scoundrels. They will deceive innumerable kindhearted people, harm themselves and others, and be disasters waiting to happen.

You need to understand that we practice because we aspire to benefit living beings through great compassion and to free them from the torments of the suffering of suffering, the suffering of conditioned existence, and the suffering of change. We do not practice to subdue spirits or demons with anger, or act mysterious and pretend to have powers.

Some people shamelessly boast, "I saw this demon today and saw that spirit yesterday, then I chanted the Vajrapani mantra and immediately I scared it away." As these people's discriminative minds that see demons and spirits become stronger, and as they praise themselves and scorn others more and more, these are signs that they are already under the influence of Mara.

If someone really possesses great love and compassion and true conviction in the Three Jewels, then even if spirits and demons pervade space and land, this person will not be harmed in any way. In particular, a person who chants the *Aspiration of Bodhisattva Samantabhadra* cannot be destroyed by evil spirits or heretics.

Besides, if you really do encounter spirits and demons, you should not wish them harm and then use all possible means to exterminate them. Instead, you should treat them with compassion and love and visualize your own body transformed into *amrita;* then offer this completely to them so they may obtain peace, happiness, and contentment. Only eradicating attachment to the self in this way can truly subdue demons.

Know that the greatest evil demon in the three realms of existence is attachment to the self. All demons and spirits are the minions of that attachment. We live day and night with this great demon king, who accompanies us like a shadow. Apart from this demon king, there is no other demon out there. Milarepa said, "If one's mind has not become a demon, then there is not a single outer demon."

Is Study or Practice More Important?

Some people now persuade everyone not to study the sutras and shastras, saying that these are meaningless and people must engage in actual practice. This is not correct. Just think—if you have never studied or contemplated, how can you really know how to practice?

If Shakyamuni Buddha were in the world, he would still ask us to first study the Dharma, then to reflect on it, and finally to practice it. Sakya Pandita also said, "Plunging into practice without having studied or reflected is like someone with a broken arm trying to climb a cliff. It is undoubtedly wishful thinking." Today, however, some "gurus" do not understand the Buddhadharma and the sutras at all, nor have they studied a single shastra in their lives. So they vehemently oppose studying and reflection, and they indiscriminately allow students to begin to practice immediately. This is the blind leading the blind, and the followers are led astray.

If they have never studied or reflected on the Buddhadharma, how do they take on disciples? If they do not even know the basic Buddhist teachings and terms, why do they tell others to not read the sutras and shastras, claiming that they themselves focus on practice and that theories are not important? These words are truly deluded and absurd!

The omniscient Longchenpa pointed out, "Only people who have mastered study and reflection can realize the ultimate Great Perfection." It is clear that if you wish to attain spiritual accomplishments, you must undertake extensive study and reflection.

I believe that in Buddhism, there is nothing more important than study and reflection. In the old days, following in the steps of Mipham Rinpoche, Lala Chudzi Rinpoche was another outstanding master. He said, "A person who is dissatisfied with people lecturing about and listening to the Buddhadharma, or unwilling to study and reflect on it themselves, is unable to attain liberation in their life. As for someone who denigrates study and reflection to attain temporary or ultimate liberation would be like a barren woman bearing a son—utterly impossible!"

Therefore, I hope that everyone will first study and reflect on the Dharma when practicing Buddhism. Otherwise, without the cause, how can the effect be produced? You will not find any precedent in the Buddhist teachings of someone who obtained wisdom without studying.

A practice devoid of study and reflection is a completely blind and aimless practice. I can guarantee that practitioners like this will not arrive at a true understanding that accords with the Buddhadharma. Nowadays, some people merely live in a quiet place and meditate all day without thinking about anything. Without the guidance of Buddhadharma's methods, even if they sit idly for five or six years, there still might not be any progress in their practice.

Do Not Wildly Claim to Fear Nothing

There are some people around me who are full of hollow words. They say things like "neither samsara nor nirvana exists"; "not grasping nor rejecting good or evil"; "I fear nothing"; and then they casually hum some tantric verses.

These people say they fear nothing, but when they encounter the slightest setback, they are seized with terror. They claim they do not grasp or reject anything, but when they meet a beautiful woman or see money, their expression instantly reveals delight. They believe themselves to be experienced practitioners, yet they never make any effort to cultivate great compassion or wisdom. They do not realize at all that these alone are the true measures of enlightenment.

Then there are those who say samsara is pure by nature; there is nothing to let go of; even if they go to hell, it matters not to them. If others call them liars when they say such things, they burst into fury and rage out of control. If you are not even scared of hell, why fear the insults of an ordinary person? You experience a chilling terror when you see even a worldly prison; the suffering in the hell realm is a million, a billion times worse. It is absolutely impossible that you do not fear it.

The truly accomplished masters indeed do not grasp or reject happiness or suffering. They do not search for buddhahood, nor do they fear samsara. But which realm of awareness do *we* actually inhabit? Surely we should know this in our heart.

Often we come across people who have cultivated a few worldly virtuous deeds, like chanting the Avalokiteshvara heart mantra one hundred million times, and they allege that they no longer fear even death. On the one hand, there is indeed inconceivable merit in cultivating virtuous deeds. But on the other hand, you should also ponder this: According to the teachings in the sutras, a single moment of anger is enough to ruin immeasurable virtue and merit. Now, how many angry thoughts have you ever had? So you should not think of yourself as being very remarkable.

I once met a monk who had quite a strong habit of speaking hollow words. I kindly advised him, "You need to take care. Your insight is not yet profound, so you should practice steadily." He did not think much of it: "It's fine! I use the prayer wheel every day. I am not scared of hell at all."

As an ordinary person, you must not think too highly of yourself. Perhaps you still like gaining, not losing; you like happiness, not suffering; you like to be praised, not insulted. You claim not to be attached to anything, but all day long you are swept around in circles by the eight worldly dharmas. If that is the case, then you are merely deceiving yourself and others.

Do Not Let Practice Become Poison

Some people think that they are free from the eight worldly dharmas and often use this "freedom" to praise themselves and denigrate others. But in fact, this act itself is the greatest worldly dharma. Their fettering by the eight worldly dharmas is in no way less than anyone else's. For instance, on the surface they refuse offerings from others, but deep down they thirst for them. The eight worldly dharmas are present here.

Some monastics are especially attached in a way that appears as if they do not wish for any respect. When others set up a Dharma throne or high seat for them, they are not willing to sit on it. Here too are the eight worldly dharmas.

In addition, when people act especially humble in front of others in order to indicate their freedom from the eight worldly dharmas, but hoping for everyone's praise—here again are the eight worldly dharmas.

Some practitioners believe they have deep insights and remarkable states of realization, then become contemptuous of others as a result. This is a poison in their practice. In contrast, there are precept-abiding practitioners who are filled with compassion when they see others break the precepts; these are practitioners in name and in fact. But if practitioners become proud of their observance of the precepts, praise themselves, and belittle others, always finding the flaws in someone else's conduct, then they are undoubtedly the true precept breakers.

There are some practitioners who appear to have renounced everything; they are not interested in worldly activities and spend years living in isolated areas to practice asceticism. But deep down, they always believe themselves to be above others; as soon as they open their mouths, derision comes out. This also is not the true mind of renunciation.

Even when you realize the true nature of mind, there still cannot be the thought, "I am enlightened." You certainly should not boast about it. When I was eighteen, I remember meeting an old man in Derge whose name was Sogyal. He appeared just like an ordinary person, and no one knew his state of realization. When he died, however, he actually attained the rainbow body.* Only then did everyone realize that he was a highly accomplished master. Thus, realizing the nature of mind does not mean it needs be readily displayed.

In reality, if you can see everything as purity and have no aversion or attachment to any phenomenon, this is the

* Rainbow body (Tib. *'ja' lus*): When a highly realized practitioner dies, the body may dissolve into rainbow light, leaving behind no corpse but only hair and nails.

ultimate enlightenment. As for those who believe they possess extraordinary wisdom and become conceited, arrogant, and contemptuous, they are not even of noble character, let alone acting cultivated.

Therefore, when we are with others, we need to carefully observe whether we are afflicted by craving, anger, delusion, envy, pride, and so forth. If we clearly see that these afflictions are deeply ingrained within us, then it means that we are not so outstanding. It also means there is a great deal of room for improvement in our practice and we must never float on cloud nine just because of some trivial states of realization!

Solitary Practice Is Dangerous

If you wish to eradicate your afflictions, you must follow your teacher and study for a long time. Otherwise, studying for only a few days will not have any significant effect.

Some people like to meditate alone in a cave or under a tree. They do not realize that this behavior is quite dangerous. It easily attracts the interference of nonhuman beings. Granted, the sutras say to practice in a quiet place. But the preconditions are that the practitioner has already followed a teacher for an extremely long time, mastered all the teachings, and eradicated all doubts. Only then may the practitioner retreat to a quiet area. Otherwise, if you have no understanding of the teachings and no sincere respect for your teacher, and you merely leave the world behind to begin practicing alone after reading a few books, then not only will there be no benefit, but there might even be danger to your life.

Before practitioners can practice in an isolated place, they must satisfy significant requirements and conditions. First, they must respect their teacher, constantly practice guru yoga, and wholeheartedly pray for their teacher's blessings. In this way they will avoid the interference of nonhuman beings. Second, they must cultivate great compassion. If they have truly aroused the bodhichitta of great compassion and loving-kindness, they are beyond the harm of any nonhuman being.

Some people today are not willing to study or reflect on the Dharma, but they are enthusiastic about meditation. They believe meditating all day with their eyes shut is the ultimate practice. I do not think much of this. Although there are people of the highest caliber who attain enlightenment without study or reflection, are you of such caliber? Therefore, you cannot live in a cave or another completely isolated place when you first start to practice. Instead, you should be with a qualified Dharma teacher and earnestly receive the Buddhadharma; it is best if you are always engaged in study, reflection, and practice. Of course, I am not asking you to study and reflect for a lifetime without ever practicing. But to spend an entire life in blind meditation without any study or reflection is also a wrong path!

Never Believe in "Forever"

In the boundless sea of samsara, even if moments of happiness appear by chance, they are merely fleeting. Like the smile of a siren, they cannot be trusted.

It is recorded in the Jataka tales that Shakyamuni Buddha was a merchant in a past life. When he traveled to the land of Locha, many sirens tempted him with myriad intrigues and sexual promises. After careful observation, however, he discovered that although they appeared extremely charming, their nature was of suffering and deceit.

The happiness in samsara is also like this. It changes from moment to moment, as evanescent as a flash of lightning. All of our possessions today—will they still be there tomorrow? Our body that is healthy today—will it still be free of illness tomorrow? None of these things can be foretold. Truly, all phenomena are like lightning.

Thus, no matter how wonderful anything in the world is, it cannot be depended upon in the least. No matter what shape or appearance it assumes, everything is inherently empty; we need not crave it. Take a banana tree: on the outside it seems so luxuriantly green, but when we peel it layer by layer, we find that the inside is completely empty, without an iota of essence.

In samsara, not a single phenomenon is worthy of trust. When good things come our way, we need not cling. When bad things come our way, we certainly need not be angry. Do not be attached to any phenomenon!

Editor's Afterword

From just a single drop of water, one can taste the flavor of the ocean. From just a single jewel-like teaching, the wondrous, exquisite nature of Buddhism can radiate. This book is not voluminous, but each word in it is a gem. The reader will savor it long after reading it.

In reality, the precious teachings from His Holiness's life are as vast as the ocean, and this book contains only a drop of it. When the causes and conditions are ripe in the future, I will translate His Holiness's other teachings and share them with those who have the affinity!

Glossary

AFFLICTIONS (Skt. *klesha;* Tib. *nyon mongs*): Mental events that arise from ignorance and cause psychological affliction. Often called "mind poisons," the five principal ones are craving, anger, delusion, pride, and envy.

AMITABHA (Skt.; Tib. *'od dpag med*): The buddha of infinite light, who presides over the pure realm of Sukhavati. One of the five dhyani buddhas.

AMRITA (Skt.; Tib. *bdud rtsi*): Divine nectar.

ARHAT (Skt.; Tib. *dgra bcom pa*): A practitioner who has realized the nonexistence of a personal self. Arhatship is the goal of the Shravakayana.

ATTAINMENT, SPIRITUAL (Skt. *siddhi;* Tib. *dngos grub*): Accomplishment that comes through meditation practice. Attainment is of two types: Ordinary attainments are worldly powers such as clairvoyance. Supreme attainment is complete enlightenment.

AVALOKITESHVARA (Skt.; Tib. *spyan ras gzigs*): The bodhisattva who embodies the compassion of all the buddhas. Known as Chenrezig in Tibetan.

BARDO (Tib.): Literally, "in between"; generally this term refers to the intermediate state between death and rebirth.

BHIKSHU (Skt.; Tib. *dge slong*): A fully ordained monk.

BODHICHITTA (Skt.; Tib. *byang chub kyi sems*): Literally, "mind of enlightenment," bodhichitta is of two types, relative and ultimate. Relative bodhichitta has two aspects: aspirational bodhichitta, which is the altruistic intention to achieve enlightenment for the sake of others, and engaged bodhichitta, which is actual engagement in the practices to accomplish this. Ultimate bodhichitta is the realization of emptiness.

BODHISATTVA (Skt.; Tib. *byang chub sems dpa'*): A Mahayana practitioner who, having given rise to bodhichitta, has vowed to attain enlightenment in order to free all sentient beings from samsara. The term encompasses ordinary beings but is particularly associated with those who have attained the enlightenment of the bodhisattva levels.

BODHISATTVA LEVELS (Skt. *bhumi;* Tib. *sa*): The ten stages of realization through which a bodhisattva progresses toward enlightenment.

DAKINI (Skt.; Tib. *mkha' 'gro*): A wrathful or semiwrathful female tantric deity.

DEPENDENT ORIGINATION (Skt. *pratityasamutpada;* Tib. *rten 'brel*): A fundamental Buddhist teaching that all phenomena lack true existence as independent entities and exist only provisionally in dependence upon the arising of causes and conditions.

DEVA (Skt.; Tib. *lha*): A god or deity.

DHARMA AGE OF DEGENERATION (Tib. *snyigs ma'i dus*): A time of spiritual degeneration such as the present age, which is said to be characterized by the spread of wrong views, the proliferation of afflictions, shortening of the life span, the physical and mental deterioration of sentient beings, and the decline of the era. *See also* Dharma age of fruition.

DHARMA AGE OF FRUITION (Tib. *'bras bu'i dus*): The time during the life of the Buddha when disciples experienced the fruition of their practice immediately. *See also* Dharma age of degeneration.

DHARMAKAYA (Skt.; Tib. *chos kyi sku*): Literally, "buddha body of reality," the ultimate nature of enlightened mind, experienced by a buddha.

DHARMA PROTECTORS (Skt. *dharmapala;* Tib. *chos skyong*): Wrathful manifestations of enlightened beings who serve to protect the teachings and practitioners from obstacles.

DZOGCHEN (Tib.): *See* Great Perfection.

EIGHT SIMILES OF ILLUSION (Tib. *sgyu ma'i dpe brgyad*): Various analogies traditionally used to illustrate the illusory nature of phenomena, including a dream, an echo, a mirage, a rainbow, a mirror's reflection, a city of celestial musicians, a magical illusion, and the image of the moon reflected in water.

EIGHT WORLDLY DHARMAS (Tib. *'jig rten chos brgyad*): The mundane concerns of pleasure and pain, gain and loss, praise and blame, and good and bad reputation.

FIELD OF MERIT (Skt. *punyakshetra;* Tib. *tshogs zhing*): The focus or object of prayers, prostrations, and other offerings. The practice of veneration of an authentic field of merit helps to generate positive qualities.

FIVE CRIMES WITH IMMEDIATE RETRIBUTION (Tib. *mtshams med lnga*): Five actions that cause one to take immediate rebirth in the hell realms after death: killing one's mother, killing one's father, killing an arhat or a more realized being, maliciously wounding a buddha, and causing a schism in the sangha.

FIVE DHYANI BUDDHAS (Skt.; Tib. *rgyal ba rigs lnga*): The buddhas of the "five families," embodying the five aspects of a buddha's wisdom: Vairochana, Akshobhya, Ratnasambhava, Amitabha, and Amoghasiddhi.

FIVE POISONS: *See* afflictions.

FIVE TRADITIONAL SCIENCES (Tib. *rigs pa'i gnas lnga*): Arts and crafts, medicine, grammar, logic, and religious philosophy.

FORTUNATE AEON (Tib. *bskal pa bzang po*): A period in which a buddha appears. Shakyamuni Buddha is the buddha of the present fortunate aeon.

GENERATION STAGE (Skt. *utpattikrama;* Tib. *bskyed rim*): Vajrayana meditation practices involving the visualization of a deity and recitation of the deity's mantra. *See also* perfection stage.

GREAT PERFECTION (Tib. *rdzogs chen*): The practice of meditation on the nature of mind. The highest teachings of the Nyingma school.

GREAT SEAL (Skt. *mahamudra;* Tib. *phag rgya chen po*): Meditation on the nature of mind, the highest teachings of the Kagyu school.

HIGHER REALMS: The realms of gods, demigods, and humans. *See also* six classes of beings.

HINAYANA (Skt.): The "Foundational Vehicle" of Buddhist teachings that emphasize the nonexistence of a personal self. The fruition of the Hinayana is arhatship.

JATAKA TALES (Skt.): Life stories of the previous incarnations of the Buddha.

KHENPO (Tib.): A title given to the abbot of a monastery or to a monk of scholarly distinction.

LOWER REALMS: The realms of animals, hungry ghosts, and hell beings. *See also* six classes of beings.

MADHYAMAKA: *See* Middle Way.

MAHAMUDRA: *See* Great Seal.

MAHASIDDHA (Skt.; Tib. *grub chen*): A yogi who has attained the supreme accomplishment of buddhahood.

MAHAYANA (Skt.; Tib. *theg pa chen po*): Literally, "Great Vehicle," the second set of teachings by the Buddha, emphasizing the emptiness of phenomena and the practice of universal compassion. The Mahayana is the path of the bodhisattva, who seeks enlightenment for the benefit of all sentient beings.

MAITREYA (Skt.; Tib. *byams pa*): The bodhisattva regent of Shakyamuni Buddha, presently residing in the heavenly realm of Tushita until becoming the fifth buddha of this aeon. He is the author of five treatises preserved by Asanga, including *Ornament of Clear Realization*.

MAJOR AND MINOR MARKS OF BUDDHAHOOD (Tib. *mtshan dang dpe byad*): The physical characteristics of a buddha, comprising thirty-two major marks (such as the ushnisha) and eighty minor marks (various qualities of his body, gait, and so on).

MANJUSHRI (Skt; Tib. *'jam dpal dbyangs*): A bodhisattva who embodies the perfection of transcendent wisdom, depicted holding a sword in one hand and a text in the other.

MARA (Skt.; Tib. *bdud*): A demon or malevolent force that creates obstacles for practice and enlightenment.

MIDDLE WAY (Skt. *madhyamaka;* Tib. *dbu ma*): A philosophical approach of the Mahayana that uses logic and reasoning to point out the emptiness of phenomena. The term is also used more generally to refer to the Buddha's path of avoiding the extremes of asceticism and overindulgence. In the context of the philosophical teachings of the Mahayana, it refers to transcending the extremes of eternalism and nihilism.

MILAREPA (Tib.) (1040–1123): A yogi who spent his life in solitary mountain hermitages and is revered throughout Tibet for his songs of realization.

NAGARJUNA (Skt.) (c. 2nd century): An Indian scholar who is renowned for his texts expounding the logical arguments for emptiness, which form the basis of the Middle Way philosophical tradition.

NOBLE BEINGS (Skt. *arya;* Tib. *'phags pa*): An epithet for enlightened beings: arhats, bodhisattvas, and buddhas.

PARINIRVANA (Skt.): The final nirvana or passing away of a buddha or great master.

PERFECTION STAGE (Skt. *sampannakrama;* Tib. *rdzogs rim*): Vajrayana meditation practiced following the dissolution of the visualization created in the development stage.

RAINBOW BODY (Tib. *'ja' lus*): When a highly realized practitioner dies, the body may dissolve into rainbow light, leaving behind no corpse but only hair and nails.

SAMSARA (Skt.; Tib. *'khor ba*): The cycle of death and rebirth characterized by ignorance and suffering, from which Buddhists seek liberation.

SANGHA (Skt.; Tib. *dge 'dun*): A community of spiritual practitioners. The term is usually used to refer to the assembly of ordained monks and nuns. *See also* Three Jewels.

SHAKYAMUNI BUDDHA (Skt.; Tib. *sha kya thub pa*): The historical Buddha of this aeon, born in India in the fifth century B.C.E.

SHASTRA (Skt.; Tib. *bstan bcos*): A commentary or philosophical treatise by a later master on the teachings of the Buddha.

SIX CLASSES OF BEINGS (Tib. *'gro ba rigs drug*): Within the desire realm, there are six realms in which one may one take birth. The realms of hell beings, hungry ghosts, and animals are the three lower realms. The realms of gods, demigods, and humans are the three higher realms.

SUKHAVATI (Skt.; Tib. *bde ba can*): The pure land of Buddha Amitabha in the west, where ordinary beings can be reborn through the power of their merit, aspiration, and bodhichitta.

SUTRAYANA (Skt.; Tib. *mdo'i theg pa*): Contrasted with the Vajrayana, the Sutrayana comprises the teachings of the Hinayana and the Mahayana.

TANTRAYANA (Skt.): *See* Vajrayana.

TATHAGATA (Skt.): Literally, "the one who has thus gone" or "the one who has thus come"; a common title for the Buddha in scripture.

TERMA (Tib.): Literally, "hidden treasure," texts by Padmasambhava that were concealed in rocks, caves, and other locations to be discovered and propagated by later masters known as *tertöns* ("treasure revealers").

TERTÖN (Tib.): *See* terma.

THREE JEWELS (Skt. *triratna;* Tib. *dkon mchog gsum*): The three objects of refuge for Buddhists: the Buddha, the Dharma, and the sangha.

THREE REALMS OF EXISTENCE (Tib. *khams gsum*): The samsaric realms of desire, form, and formlessness.

TONGLEN (Tib.): Literally, "sending and taking," a meditation practice designed to develop compassion and diminish attachment to the self, in which one visualizes taking on the suffering and wrongdoing of others and sending them one's own happiness and virtue.

TRIPITAKA (Skt.; Tib. *sde snod gsum*): Literally, "three baskets," the three collections of Buddhist scripture: (1) the vinaya, or rules of monastic conduct; (2) the sutras, or discourses of the Buddha; and (3) the abhidharma, or teachings on phenomenology and epistemology.

TULKU (Tib.): A lama or teacher who is a reincarnation of a previous master.

USHNISHA (Skt.): The protuberance on the crown of a buddha's head, usually oval-shaped in Buddhist iconography.

VAJRAYANA (Skt.; Tib. *rdo rje theg pa*): A branch of the Mahayana based on the tantras, employing skillful means that bring a quick result. Also called Tantrayana.

About the Author

His Holiness Jigme Phuntsok Rinpoche (1933–2004) was a prominent teacher in the Nyingma tradition of Tibetan Buddhism and a master of the Great Perfection. He was recognized as a *tertön* (treasure revealer) and an incarnation of Sogyal Lerab Lingpa, a teacher to the Thirteenth Dalai Lama. His Holiness was renowned for his consummate skill in communicating the Dharma and remarkably personable and compassionate spiritual leadership. Unlike many Tibetan masters who fled to India and the West, His Holiness remained in China throughout the Cultural Revolution and played a major role in maintaining and reviving Buddhism in the region. In 1980, he established a nonsectarian Buddhist community called Larung Gar near the town of Serthar in China's Sichuan Province, where he taught a diverse student body of thousands—including monks, nuns, and laypeople. The Larung Gar Five Sciences Buddhist Academy continues today and is one of the largest and most influential centers of Buddhist learning in the world.

About the Editor

KHENPO SODARGYE RINPOCHE is one of the primary leaders of the Larung Gar Five Sciences Buddhist Academy founded by His Holiness Jigme Phuntsok Rinpoche. He was His Holiness's chief Chinese translator and one of his closest students. Like His Holiness, Khenpo is widely respected for his extraordinary spiritual leadership and ability to make the Dharma accessible to students of many levels and backgrounds, including groundbreaking efforts to support the transmission of Buddhism with new media and technologies. He has traveled extensively to the United States, Canada, Germany, France, Holland, the United Kingdom, and throughout Asia to offer teachings, and he continues to teach widely at schools and universities worldwide. He is considered one of the most important and influential Tibetan Buddhist teachers in China today. For more information about Khenpo Sodargye and his work, visit www.khenposodargye.org.